Graphic Design
BASICS

Creating
Logos &
Letterheads

Jennifer Place

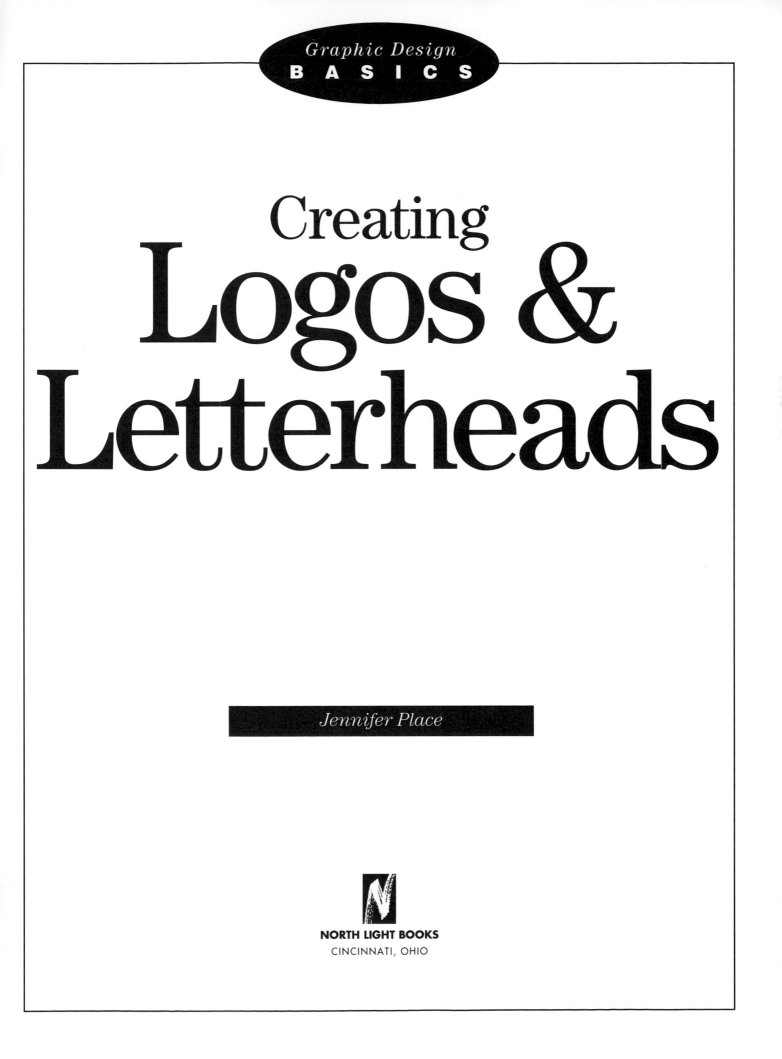

NORTH LIGHT BOOKS
CINCINNATI, OHIO

Printed and bound in the United States of America.

This hardcover edition of *Creating Logos & Letterheads* features a "self-jacket" that
eliminates the need for a separate dust jacket. It provides sturdy protection for your
book while it saves paper, trees and energy.

Other fine North Light Books are available from your local bookstore, art supply
store or direct from the publisher.

99 98 97 96 95   5 4 3 2 1

Library of Congress Cataloging-in-Publication Data

Place, Jennifer.
    Creating logos & letterheads / by Jennifer Place. — 1st ed.
        p. cm. — (Graphic design basics)
    Includes index.
    ISBN 0-89134-571-X (alk. paper)
    1. Logotype—Design. 2. Letterheads—Design. I. Title
II. Series.
NC1002.L63P57 1995
741.6—dc20
                                                    95-1851
                                                    CIP

Edited by Lynn Haller and Terri Boemker
Designed by Angela Lennert
Cover illustration by Angela Lennert

The permissions on page iii constitute an extension of this copyright page.

About the Author

Jennifer Place has her own company, Place Design. Educated in fine
art at Bennett College and New York University, she began her career
as a book editor, working with step-by-step arts and crafts books at
Watson-Guptill Publications. This led to freelance writing for various
magazines about the same subjects. Her work with books involved all
processes—organizing, editing, writing and designing. But after six
years of company life, she left her position as a senior editor in book
development, moved to Canada, and spent three and a half years being
an artist. There, two Toronto galleries showed her prints and work on
paper regularly. A return to the States (landing in Hoboken, New
Jersey) prompted another change in career direction, and it was at
that point that she started Place Design, specializing in book design
and production. Not one to keep her hand entirely out of the writing
business, however, Ms. Place has coauthored books such as *Color in
Architecture and Interior Design*, *Country Crafts* and *Country
Quilts*. Her mixed-media sculpture has been shown at various galleries
and spaces in New York and New Jersey. She is on the Board of
Directors of the Hudson Waterfront Museum and on the Board of
Advisors of the Hoboken Division of Cultural Affairs.

Acknowledgments

This book would not have happened if I hadn't gone on my yearly trek
to Maine, to visit my friend Margit Malmstrom, where I met Val
Adkins, who was writing another book in this Graphic Design Basics
series: *Creating Brochures & Booklets*. Val called her editor, Mary
Cropper, and said that she'd shanghaied another writer who might be
interested in doing a book for the series. And two years later I'm still
typing! Thank you all.

    This book would be half its size if not for my wonderful editor,
Lynn Haller, who kept saying, "Write more; we need more!" She asked
just the right questions, made insightful comments, and campaigned
just hard enough when the deadlines started slipping. Thanks also to
Terri Boemker and Bruce Stoker, who pulled all the pieces together in
a final round of editing and production.

    The book is much improved by the designer-friends who generous-
ly donated their time and their work to create examples or demonstrations, notably Mark Campbell, Geri Fallo, Anthony Ferrara, Jill
Willinger, McKevin Shaugnessy, David Sadowski and Helena Guzzy.
Thanks also go to all the designers and printers who gave permission
for their work to be used as examples throughout the text and in the
gallery chapter.

    The book would have been done faster if I didn't have a dog that
needed walking for hours every day—thanks, Frank—but then again,
those walks gave me time to think, and that's the first step toward getting any work done at all.

Permissions

Contents

Chapter Three: Business Card Design

Like stationery, business cards are used by virtually every business. In this chapter, you'll learn how to create business cards that not only provide information, but do it in a way that gets your card noticed, kept, filed—and used.

Chapter Four: Business Form Design

This chapter shows you how to design business forms that are clear, useable, attractive—and a continuation of your client's identity.

Chapter Five: More Good Examples

Look here to discover all the different ways you can design a stationery system to stand out from the rest. Each of these pieces is unique, but more importantly, each piece spotlights the client or individual it was created for.

Chapter Six: Printing Basics

In this chapter, you'll learn the basics of going from design to final printed piece. Make sure that you and your printer are speaking the same language so you can get the results you want.

Index

Introduction

Whether you're working for yourself or for a company, the most common items you'll be asked to design, especially if your client is a start-up company, are the pieces that this book covers—logos, letterheads, business cards and business forms. Together, these elements form the foundation of virtually every company's identity system; every business needs them, and even companies that already have a stationery system will need it redesigned or updated from time to time.

But how do you begin to design something that has to both express identity and serve a useful purpose? How do you know whether a graphic or a name-based logo is more appropriate for your client? What kind of paper should you pick for your letterhead? What do you do when you're designing one element but you don't have the go-ahead—or the budget—to redesign the rest of the system? What if the image your piece needs to express calls for engraving but you can't afford it?

This book is designed to answer these questions and many more—in fact, almost every question a beginning designer might have about designing any of these pieces, whether as a whole system or as just one component. The information is divided up according to the piece being designed so that, if you need some inspiration in designing a business form, you don't have to read through lots of material to find what you need—just open to the chapter on business form design. The chapters are also chock-full of tips and examples that will inspire even more experienced designers to rethink designing these old standards in a new way.

Each chapter is also designed for quick reference—beginning with the basic information you need to start designing that specific piece (complete, when possible, with lists of tips that should be great idea starters) and then followed by two to five demonstrations showing these basic principles in action. These demonstrations let you watch a designer at work, from the beginning of a project to the final printed piece. One project is also carried through from chapter to chapter to show how a logo is designed, then becomes part of the design of each component—letterhead, envelope, business card and invoice.

After each element is covered in its own chapter, there is a section of excellent examples of stationery systems showing how other designers work within the parameters of these formats to come up with great designs. Finally, the last chapter tells you how to prepare any of these pieces for the printer.

My aim in this book is to provide you with all the basic information you need to design any of these pieces and to fully understand both the limitations and the possibilities within these formats. And armed with this foundation, you are then free to do what started you designing in the first place—to get creative.

Chapter One
Logo Design

A well-executed logo embodies the spirit and character of a company. It is "instant identity," a way of capturing how companies feel about themselves and conveying that image to the outside world.

Pictorial symbols have existed throughout the history of humankind—from the pictographs used by prehistoric people to the visual insignia used to represent families in the Middle Ages. But, it was not until the Industrial Revolution that the use of brand names, labels and trademarks became widespread.

Today, everybody from small businesses to huge corporations uses a logo. They still connote value; in fact, major brand names, and their accompanying logos, are powerful commodities in the business world. A logo represents a certain level of quality and service, and the brand loyalty and development of public trust generated by this logo in turn helps to ensure the reliability of the company and its products. The company logo, in many cases, can become almost as important as the company's product or service.

Obviously, logos are not to be taken lightly; they're the foundation of a company's identity system and need to be carefully designed with an eye for communication and flexibility. But that doesn't mean a logo can't be inventive and fun, too. This chapter will show you how to achieve both.

Learn how to design a logo that catches the eye and engages the mind.

Types of Logos

There are three basic types of logos. The first is a typographic or decorative treatment of a person's or company's name or initials; the second is a graphic logo that uses a symbol or shape to represent the person or company. The third type of logo—and many successful logos fall into this category—combines both these approaches in one design.

Many of the best-known logos are name-based. This type of logo is especially effective if the name is short, such as Ford, or distinctive, such as Coca-Cola or L'eggs. If the name of the company is made up of several words, it may be preferable to use the initials instead, as in the case of IBM, originally known as International Business Machines. Type logos can be set in a distinctive face (in the business world, letterforms are often created or altered just for a logo), and the type can be colored, shadowed or otherwise manipulated.

Graphic logos use a symbol or shape to represent a company; Bell Telephone's simple bell shape and Mercedes Benz's "star" are typical examples. This type of logo is often recognizable without the company name, and some examples of this type of logo, such as the red cross used by the International Red Cross, are so well-known that they are recognized worldwide. Sometimes—especially in the case of smaller, more informal businesses—these symbols pictorially represent what the company does, but more often they symbolize some facet of the company; CBS's eye, for instance, symbolizes the fact that CBS is watched.

Other graphic logos are quite abstract, but even these logos may still imply a trait of the company, such as

The name of this company, Roundabout, lends itself to a clever typographical treatment that expresses the meaning of the word.

This logo, a typical example of a realistic graphic logo, would work with or without the name of the company to say something about the nature of the business—in this case, a coffee house.

A completely abstract logo can be created with logo-making software—in this case, using Logo Super-Power from Decathlon Corporation. A graphic effect is layered over a base shape and each is modified in terms of line weight, position and so on.

Initials can be made into a logo by using color, texture or graphic elements. This logo for Armstrong's Graphic Team uses lowercase serif initials set askew against a background of geometric shapes.

Many logos combine both a visual and a name; in this case, the initials become the acronym by which the company is known. Designer: Mark Campbell.

strength, solidity or movement; other examples of this type of logo can be very stylized, abstract versions of an earlier figurative logo that has evolved over time. The Shell Oil graphic, for example, evolved from a rather realistic rendering of a seashell to the more abstract shell design used today. Whatever their origins, abstract logos often look quite similar to one another; it can be difficult to be unique or distinctive if you choose to go this route.

Combination logos, in which a typographic treatment of a name is combined with an icon or some form of artwork, are very common. A designer may choose this type of logo because the client wants a graphic symbol for her logo but feels it's important to include the name or initials along with the graphic. Or a designer may use the combination logo to work with more than one interesting facet of the company or person. In some cases it may be crucial to include the name in the logo (this can be especially significant in the case of start-up businesses that are just beginning to make themselves known in their community), while in other cases the name might be only a secondary feature.

Deciding which type of logo is best for each project depends on such factors as the company's name, business and self-image. For instance, a typographical treatment is a logical choice for a company with a distinctive name or for a business whose name is also the name of the owner, while either a typographic logo or an abstract symbol will work for a company whose business is hard to illustrate (as in the case of a conglomerate) or for a company whose image—or whose business itself—is very serious. Other businesses, such as retail or restaurant establishments with a casual image, naturally lend themselves to a logo made from a pictograph or illustration. Logos can convey or depict a feeling, a lifestyle, a career or a hobby; they can be based on an environment, a color or a favorite thing. In designing a logo, the endless possibilities are both a difficulty and a challenge.

Designing a Logo

Before starting a logo project, you'll need to get some background information. You can start by asking yourself the following questions:

• Does your client already have some ideas about what he or she wants from this new logo? Corporate clients might have a color or a typeface that you must use, while individuals or small businesses might want their logo to have a certain flavor that relates to their self-image.

• Is there a previous version of a logo to use as a point of departure or other pieces of printed matter that must be matched?

• What is your client's budget? How much design time can your client afford? How many colors will the logo be printed in? Will your client want (and be able to afford) to incorporate special effects, such as die-cutting or embossing?

• What is the end use of this logo? If it will be used on packaging or signage as well as printed pieces, the logo will need to be flexible enough to work at several different sizes or with a variety of different color treatments.

After you've answered all of these questions, you can begin the next stage of the process: generating a large number of ideas. There are two primary ways to start brainstorming visual ideas: sketching them by hand and sketching them on the computer.

Sketching by hand will help you get ideas down fast, making it easy to explore a variety of options without getting hung up on the details; on the downside, you'll have to start from scratch if you decide to create your

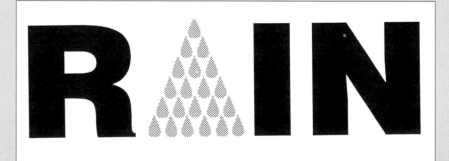

To brainstorm ideas for a name-based logo, pick a word and set it in a variety of typefaces: thick, thin, plain and fancy. Then think about which faces begin to fit the meaning of the word or which can be graphically altered to make a good logo. As you can see in this example, different typefaces can give a completely different flavor to the word they're used for; compare the formality of Caslon Open Face (second, in the middle column) to the casual feel lent by Freestyle Script (fourth, in the middle column). Even variations of the same typeface can differ somewhat in feel, as shown by the right-hand column, all of which are variations of Helvetica. In the case of this logo, I ended up choosing Helvetica Black for the final logo because its simplicity ensured that it wouldn't vie for attention with the teardrops illustration I chose to substitute for the A.

To brainstorm ideas for a graphic logo, pick a visual item—in this case, a leaf—and draw it in as many ways as you can think of. The sketches (at the top) were done in pencil, but you could try experimenting further by drawing with different mediums, colors and styles to get an even wider variety of results. The sketches (at the bottom) were developed on the computer; as you can see, it was easy for me to change the tones, line weights and effects in my drawing program to achieve a variety of results. The images obtained using the computer are crisp and accurate, but the hand-sketched versions offer more spontaneous, softer results.

final artwork on the computer.

Sketching by computer will result in very tight, accurate sketches and will make it easy for you to manipulate shapes, colors and type. You can even use very simple computer programs to create "instant logos" by imposing an effect or texture on a background shape. You can use these programs to brainstorm very effectively, changing images and colors very fast. Computer sketching does have drawbacks: The limitations of the program you're working with may limit you, and some designers feel that logos that have been completely computer generated have an indistinctive, "canned" look.

To develop a logo from a name, start by experimenting with the letters themselves. Pick a name (or another word) and play with it; you'll begin to see all the things that can happen just by using type. Try setting the word using all the variations of one typeface. Condense and expand the type; use different effects, such as drop shadows or color fills. Use different typefaces. Reverse the type, put it in a box or in a circle. Now study the results and see which effects actually begin to visually convey the content of your word.

If you don't have access to a computer, get some type sample books from the library, from a graphic arts store or directly from type distributors. Or you can explore books on calligraphy or old books on sign making or lettering for ideas for type treatments. Sketch the letterforms freehand, by tracing or by using a photocopier to enlarge or reduce the letters and then cutting and pasting. Use pencil, markers or brushes for different effects. When you have what

Designing a Logo

you want, you can have the words typeset professionally. Or you can cheaply "typeset" the logo yourself by using press-on lettering, stencils, rubber stamps or woodblocks. Also keep in mind that hand-lettering can be a beautiful option all by itself or in combination with typesetting.

Names expressed with initials are both a type and a graphic challenge. You can choose a beautiful typeface, then alter the letterspace or letterforms to make the initials unique, for a classic approach, or you can combine or overlap the letterforms to form interesting shapes. Or you can turn one or more of the letters into a geometric shape; for example, an *A* easily turns into a triangle, an *O* into a circle, and so on. There may be a representational tie-in; for instance, if the logo included the initial *O*, and the company manufactured sporting goods, the *O* could be a baseball.

Developing a purely graphic logo is similar to developing a name-based logo: Take whatever you have to start with—a previous logo, an image, a shape or color, or an idea—and start to play with it. For example, pick a real visual—say, a leaf—and sketch it in several different ways, starting off with more realistic treatments and becoming more abstract. Draw in different mediums, with your other hand, or with your eyes closed. Put the object in a box or a circle; reverse the piece. Keep going. The more you manipulate the image, the more ideas you'll generate.

The process of developing a combination logo, however, varies somewhat from the two approaches outlined above. It may happen that you've developed the graphic first but then decided that it isn't quite

Here are some hand-drawn comps for a company that transfers European videos into an American format; the client wanted to project a global image. The designer worked with both literal and abstract representations of the globe, combining these with various type treatments. As you can see, the designer was able to emulate these typefaces quite accurately with pencil sketches. (Designer: Jill Willinger.)

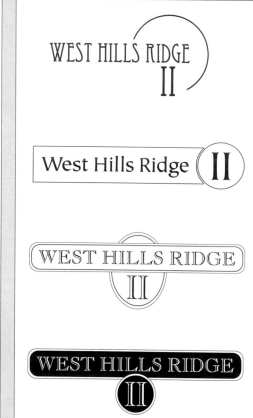

These comps were done on the computer for the typographical logo of a real estate development company. They are very accurate in type, color and graphics. If printed out with high resolution, computer comps like these could also be used as final art ready for printing. (Designer: Anthony J. Ferrara.)

Here is the evolution of an abstract logo, from initial sketches to the final version, which was developed from the name of the company. Seaport Orthopaedic Associates is a long name, so I started by playing with the initials. It is also a misleading name, since the word seaport refers to their location rather than their practice. The client wanted an abstract icon that would blend with the avant-garde type treatment of their name. At the top of the page are my hand-drawn sketches showing various combinations of initials, most groupings either touching or overlapping in some way. Below that are four sketches that I actually showed to the client, who chose the logo on the far left. I then refined the logo several times, using different combinations of white, black and gray. Immediately above is the final logo with type in place. This logo was used not only on their stationery, but also on mugs, as a wall plaque and in a newsletter.

enough to fully represent the company, so you've included a type treatment of the name or initials to complement the graphic. Or, in working with a typographic logo, you may have developed a complementary image that makes a more complete logo than the type would alone.

No matter what kind of logo you're developing, your next step after you've made initial sketches will be selecting several for further refinement. Spread your sketches out on a table and take a critical look at them. Which ones catch your eye? Which seem to work for your particular needs or client? Which seem strong and focused? There are usually two or three ideas in any group of sketches that lend themselves to "comps"—more refined versions of your original sketches. You can do comps in pencil, pen or marker, or by computer. The difference between the comp and previous versions of the logo is that your sketch now reflects all the elements of the logo in the right proportion and with more specific details. The lettering looks like the actual typeface; you've indicated the colors. Your proportion, scale and graphic elements are now crisp and accurate.

After you and your client have evaluated the comps and chosen the final version, and after you've made any final corrections or changes to the logo, you'll need to prepare the actual artwork for the printer; see chapter six for detailed instructions on preparing mechanicals for printing and color processes.

Project 1: A Type-Based Logo

The Client: Mid-Atlantic Food Distributors, Inc., is a packager of meat products. It began ten years ago with the name Mid-Atlantic Beef and with a logo that conveyed the company's business literally—with a steer head. The combination of the name of the company, the description underneath and the logo said exactly what the company did, but with a style that was dated and an image that firmly connected the company to beef products exclusively.

While still primarily involved in beef products, the company now processes, packages and distributes poultry, seafood and processed meats as well as beef. The name change, to Mid-Atlantic Food Distributors, Inc., reflected the expansion and also provided the motivation to develop a new graphic image.

The owner wanted a new logo that was modern and colorful and that didn't limit the types of food the company dealt with. He asked Anthony Ferrara, the designer, for an image that was more high-tech, and while the steer head was clearly an image that could be updated and made quite interesting, he wanted to depart from this former beefy identity. The company planned to develop a new logo that was flexible enough to be applied on a small scale to letterhead, envelopes, business cards, packaging and labels, as well as on a larger scale to shipping cartons and trucks.

Step 1. Anthony began by sketching logo ideas in pencil—from the literal to the very abstract. Since the new name of the company is very long, he focused on the company's initials—particularly the M and the A, whose strong shapes had the potential to combine with the name into an interesting logo. He started by combining the initial M with a stylized animal image to come up with a more modern, iconographic version of the old steer-head logo. Further experiments related the initials to the trucking or transportation industry, using directional arrows to imply movement or shipping. He was striving for a logo that combined the high-tech image the client desired with the spirit of the meatpacking industry. Other sketches resembled a brand or tag, an image that would complement the rugged image of the business. The concept for the logo therefore evolved into one that would be a mark or "brand" that would not just be specific to one animal and that would summarize all the different food products.

Step 2. Anthony next turned to the computer to refine the strongest of his initial sketches. He typeset the initial M, using strong, heavy typefaces such as Bodega, Black Oak, Meta, Gothic Thirteen and Futura. The first logo cuts the initial in half; the next attaches the M to a circular border and simply runs the company name beneath the logo. This kept the type treatment of the name very simple so the initial would remain the strongest image. A further refinement cuts the circle into two semicircles.

The Assignment: Redesign a logo for a company whose business has changed and expanded.

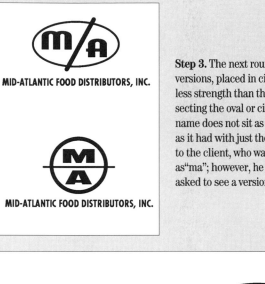

Step 3. The next round of sketches used both the M and the A. These versions, placed in circle and oval shapes and bisected by a rule, have less strength than the solid M but show balance and containment. Bisecting the oval or circle in various ways adds graphic interest. The name does not sit as comfortably under these round shapes, however, as it had with just the letter M. Anthony showed this round of sketches to the client, who was concerned that the letters M and A would read as"ma"; however, he liked the solidity of the M in the semicircles, so he asked to see a version using all three initials.

Step 4. Anthony then applied the three initials to the previous logo versions and again showed them to the client. The first logo shown (at top) in step 2, using strong type with the name bisecting a large M, evolved into three letters with the name beneath. This treatment was rejected because it was just not interesting enough. The second version, based on the M in the circle, has more visual interest: The length of the letters necessitated using a wide oval rather than a circle, with the letters attached in a striking way. The third version—the one the client ended up choosing—was based on step 2's split circle, which the client had liked to begin with; in this version, the letters were now reversed in a smaller oval, and the line thickness of the second oval lightened. The name sat well underneath the oval shape, and the result is strong and "brand-like."

Step 5. In this final version, Anthony modified the type slightly so it would sit comfortably in the oval. He also added bullets between the letters to make the logo read even more like initials rather than a word. The designer picked two colors, a dusky blue and a very dark green, and gave the client three or four different paper samples to look at. The client preferred the recycled white stock and wanted to use the dark green, not the blue, for the logo and a very dark gray for the type.

Specifications:

Designer: Anthony J. Ferrara

Type:
 Initials: Black Oak
 Spelled-out name: Meta Normal

Hardware: Macintosh IICi

Software: Adobe Illustrator, QuarkXPress

Colors: PMS 408 dark gray and PMS 568 forest green

Paper stock: French Speckletone True White Text and Cover

Clever ways to make logos from initials:

- Use a textured drop shadow behind the letters.

- Place the top or bottom half of the initials in a reverse or colored box.

- Draw a fine line around each of the initials.

- Use a different typeface for each initial.

- Remove parts of each letter, such as the cross piece of an A or the diagonal of a Z.

- Put each letter in a different colored square or box.

Project 2: A Graphic Logo

The Client: Pink House Design, a small company owned and operated by Patricia Smith, specializes in the design and execution of period gardens. The client's interest in classical flora and fauna grew from having lived in, and landscaped, a Federal farmhouse and from now owning the small Victorian home pictured at right. Starting with her own environment, Patricia researched the plants that were cultivated in yesteryear's gardens and took classes at a nearby botanical garden and research center; her personal interests slowly became a business when others began to ask her for help with their gardens. The name of the company comes from her own home, which, though it is now painted pale pink, was a much brighter pink when she bought it and was therefore known locally as "the pink house."

At first, Patricia went to her local print shop for a quick business card. Then, as the business grew, she realized she needed a whole set of printed materials with a cohesive look, not just a card. The distinctive name of the company lent itself to some sort of realistic graphic logo rather than just a type treatment. She wanted the logo to be old-fashioned, though not particularly Victorian, in flavor and to incorporate the house as well as some landscape elements.

Step 1. In one of my visits to the client, I asked for a photo of the house to use as a starting point.

Step 2. I knew that I wanted to use an image of the house as part of the logo. CorelDRAW includes a variety of architectural symbols, so I picked a house symbol that had some of the elements I knew I needed—windows, doors, and so on. I placed this symbol on the page at a size of about 1/2", then used the "break apart" command to make each one of the elements a separate item; this way, I could manipulate each one to the size and shape I wanted, starting with the windows, then the house shape and door elements. I drew the details over the windows with the pen tool, sizing and shaping them to fit the two different window styles. It took a bit of patience to get the shape of the house just right, but if you compare the last drawing to the photo in step 1, you'll see the resemblance is pretty close.

 Creating Logos & Letterheads

The Assignment: Create a logo for a garden design company based on a pink Victorian house in the country.

Step 3. At this point I didn't know quite how I wanted to treat the drawing I had made. It wasn't enough just to add colors, as this drawing didn't have the old-fashioned look I wanted. I decided to do some research, looking at books of old architectural drawing, Victorian design and gardens. Eventually I found this tiny woodcut ornament. It had the right flavor, and I felt I could alter my drawing of the house to have the same feel as this ornament.

Step 4. I enlarged the house drawing and printed it out, then experimented with various ways of layering the lines so it looked like a woodcut, which is actually a reverse image, where the white areas are cut away and the blacks are the uncarved portion of the wood. I felt I was coming close enough to the look I wanted simply by using a marker to thicken the lines. Drawing freehand on scratchboard (board coated with a black surface that you scrape away) would have been another way to create this woodcut effect, but I already had the computer image to work with, and creating the image on paper rather than scratchboard made the image easier to scan.

Step 5. It took several tries to get the image you see here. (All along, I kept using the photocopier to reduce the drawing so I could see what it would look like on the smaller scale at which it would eventually be printed.) Once I got a final image that satisfied me, I scanned it so I could return to the computer for the rest of the design.

Specifications:

Hardware: PC 386, Hewlett-Packard ScanJet II

Software: Aldus PageMaker, Corel-DRAW

Ways to use realistic images to create a logo:

- Use the image in a tint as a background device.

- Have a child draw the thing you want as a logo.

- Change a photo of something to a drawing.

- Use a portion of an old map in a ruled box.

- Trace and repeat an image.

- Silhouette an image and reproduce it upside down or sideways.

- Use a familiar image in an unfamiliar pattern or color.

- Redraw an image in an unexpected medium.

Project 2: A Graphic Logo

Step 6. Now it was time to add some landscape elements to the house—an especially important component because of the nature of my client's business. My first attempt was to photocopy some bushes and trees from a book of woodcuts and engravings, which I placed on either side of the house I had already created. If these had worked out well, I could have scanned this whole image, but I was not pleased with the results I got with this method—as you can see, this shrubbery was too intricate in style for the house I had already created.

Step 7. I then turned to a clip art file of woodcuts created for the computer, which included a number of trees and shrubs that I thought would work better with the house.

Step 8. I printed out the clip art trees and shrubs at approximately the same scale as my last version of the house, then cut and tried some samples with the house logo I had done. Then I decided which shrubs I liked and did some re-touching with white paint to simplify the foliage a bit so it would fit around the house shape and "read" better when reduced.

Step 9. I scanned the retouched shrubs so I could add them to the scanned image of the house on the computer. This way, I had a complete, scalable computer logo to place on any future layouts. I applied color at this stage as well—pink, of course, for the house and a grayish dark green for the shrubs (chapter two shows the logo in color and placed on the letterhead). This logo works both in black and white and in color, and it can stand alone or work well with accompanying type.

Chapter Two
Stationery Design

The combination of letterhead and envelope is a powerful promotional tool. While it is the most utilitarian, and probably most ubiquitous, component of a company's identity system, it is also a fairly cost-efficient way to convey the fundamental qualities of a company or individual—its philosophy, spirit, intelligence and ability. As with a company's logo, when stationery elements are well thought out and designed, they can be a great vehicle for visually expressing a company's character and imagination.

A good stationery design exploits this promotional opportunity by taking into account what the individual or company wants to convey, then balancing this with more practical considerations. For instance, is the stationery so expensive and elaborate that everyone's afraid to use it? Does it have such a small area for actual written messages that the briefest correspondence takes up three pages? Is the paper so delicate that your laser printer mangles every page? Is the style so trendy that it looks dated after three months of use? If the answer to any of these questions is yes, you need to reconsider your design. Always keep in mind that the best letterhead design balances practical and aesthetic goals to arrive at a piece that's both appropriate and appealing.

Stationery is an everyday item—but it doesn't have to be ordinary. Learn how to make sure yours is unique.

Planning and Layout

Before starting to design a piece of stationery, you must consider what information it needs to include, what elements you have to start with, who will use it, and who will receive it. Your first step will be to gather from the client all the information that must be included on the letterhead. Letterhead usually includes the company's or individual's name, address, telephone number and fax number, but it may also include a list of board members, company divisions, or a variety of other information. The standard envelope includes at least the name and address, but it may include additional information or even a logo.

Then you need to know what graphic elements, if any, the client has in mind. Is there an existing logo or type treatment that you must use? Are there certain colors already associated with the company? Is there an existing letterhead that is out-of-date? If so, does the client want a revision or an entirely new treatment? If you are starting from scratch, does the client have specific ideas—a color scheme or type of paper (for example, recycled paper)—that must be used in the final piece? The answers to these questions are the beginning of your design.

Next consider how the person or company will use the letterhead. Will it be printed, or will it exist only on the computer? Are messages to be handwritten (as they would be for personal stationery), or will they be done on a computer, word processor or typewriter? Does the client's office equipment have trouble handling any specific types of paper? If the paper stock or a background design is in color, how will corrections in the typed material be made (on comput-

Conventional letterhead layouts, like the ones shown here, typically use type and elements that are centered, flush left or flush right, and toward the top or bottom of the page.

Unconventional letterhead layout can break all the rules, placing type and graphics in all sorts of positions, while still leaving room for the actual letter.

er, with correction fluid, etc.)? Will the letterhead regularly be faxed or photocopied? If so, you should avoid picking a dark or heavily flecked stock, as it would take far too long to fax and would be illegible when photocopied.

The other side of this equation—and another factor to consider when designing letterhead—is who will receive the letterhead. The design of the piece needs to be appropriate to its market. Is this personal stationery that needs to be intimate or striking? Is it corporate letterhead that will function as a sales tool? What is the company's personality: Should its letterhead shout or whisper? What colors, graphics and typefaces will appeal to those who will be receiving this letterhead?

Size is another factor to determine at the beginning. The standard letterhead size is 8 ½" x 11", which folds in thirds to fit into a standard business-size envelope. The 7 ¼" x 10 ½" monarch size is traditionally used by executives, and personal notepaper can be smaller as well, folding in half to fit into a squarish envelope. When choosing a size, keep in mind that the laser printers used in most offices will usually let you go narrower than an 8 ½" x 11" sheet, but they generally won't let you go wider.

Also keep in mind that certain design treatments may affect the way the job needs to be handled by the printer. For example, a printer will consider type or color elements that bleed off the page or come close to the margin to be an oversize job that needs a larger sheet of paper and trimming, and they will charge accordingly.

Once all of these issues have been considered, you can think about the

Planning and Layout

layout. There are certain parameters within which you'll need to work when designing a piece of stationery. The information included needs to be readable and sequential. There should be a balance between graphic innovation and practical use; i.e., the graphic elements shouldn't be so intrusive that the stationery is impossible to use. The actual space needed for use will usually be at least 80 percent of the whole page, and that space needs to be completely intact; the information probably won't, for instance, divide the page in half, unless your market is really offbeat and the people who will be using the stationery are unusually patient.

There are various tried-and-true layouts for an 8 ½" x 11" piece of stationery. The most traditional of these options, such as having the type centered across the top or bottom of the page or placed in a bar on the left-hand margin of the page, work because they are readable, logical, easy to use, and leave maximum space for the actual letter. If you use this kind of layout, the reader will immediately know where to find the necessary information. A conventional layout is also a good choice if you're planning other special effects, such as really unconventional type or marbled blue vellum paper.

Choosing a more innovative solution to letterhead layout—running the type up the side vertically or around in a circle— can also be an effective choice, depending on the client's business and market. For instance, while a legal office probably shouldn't have stationery with type running around in a spiral, that might be an appropriate solution for an innovative music studio with a young or

Historic references and graphics can be a great starting point for letterhead layout. These examples include layouts inspired by (from top left, clockwise) the 1920s, 1950s, 1930s and the Victorian era.

Creating Logos & Letterheads

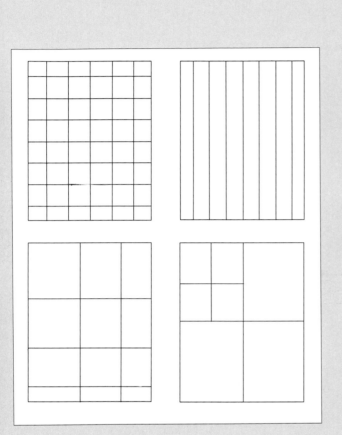

Working with a grid will give your letterhead an instant structure. A grid can be as simple as an allover checkerboard pattern or columns of equal width (top) to more complex patterns that make use of areas of unequal size (bottom).

offbeat client base. An unconventional layout is also useful for spicing up a one-color job on less expensive paper. Even specifying an unusual placement of copy on the letterhead—perhaps with the use of subtle icons or rules to guide those using the letterhead—can serve as a way to create a unique letterhead layout.

After you've got the necessary background information and have thought about what general type of layout is most appropriate for your piece, you're ready to start planning the layout itself. Begin by doing some small sketches with a thick pencil or marker, just roughing out where the various elements might go in the rectangle. Indicate in a similar way the logo or other graphics.

You might want to work with a grid to help position your elements, especially if you have to carry the letterhead design through to other pieces, such as a business card, envelope or label. While grids are often thought of in conjunction with laying out publication pages, using a grid to help with other kinds of layouts is a good idea. A grid affords instant structure—organizing your margins, type and graphics—as well as providing consistency between pieces. Grids can be used to divide space or to ensure the proportion of elements. A grid can change proportionally to suit the size of the piece, with the elements changing along with it. A grid can also be as simple or as complicated as the project requires—from one that's as simple as a checkerboard pattern to a grid that splits the page into various areas, each having its own pattern to follow. See project 3 on pages 48-51 to see an example of how to use a simple grid to design a layout.

Variations for letterhead layouts:

- Make lines of type fit into a geometric shape.

- Bleed large type off the top or bottom of the page.

- Consider making use of a grid to help position your elements, especially if you need to carry the letterhead design through to other pieces.

- Change the color, shape or position of elements from one piece to another in a system.

- Use reverse layouts on the letterhead and on the envelope, such as reversing the position of the type and logo or reversing the colors.

Selecting Type

Like the layout, the type treatment you choose for a piece of letterhead will be influenced by the information you have to start with. A client may ask for a particular type treatment or may have a particular look in mind. If there is a logo but no existing type treatment for a company, it might be a simple matter of choosing an appropriate typeface, ink color and paper stock and using a simple layout.

Also keep in mind that your choice of typeface should not conflict with whatever typeface the company normally uses for the body of its correspondence. Some companies are casual about what typefaces can be used in the body of their letters, but others—particularly very large corporations or more visual or creative businesses—are fairly strict in prescribing a consistent typeface to be used for all correspondence. Find out which category your client belongs to before selecting type for the letterhead.

Type designed for text falls into two different categories: serif and sans serif. Serif faces evolved from hand-lettering, where the pen left little edges at the end of a stroke as it left the paper; this characteristic was refined and reinterpreted in a variety of ways by early type designers. Sans serif type—a relatively modern development in type design—simplifies each letter by eliminating those ornamental details, giving a more monotone quality to a block of copy, as well as usually being more compact than serif faces. Either kind of text type is an appropriate choice for large blocks of type or for any type that must be readable.

When you're using only a small amount of type, you also have the op-

Avant Garde
Futura
Grotesque
Xavier Sans
Baskerville
Cheltenham
Galliard
Novarese

Typical sans serif typefaces include Avant Garde, Futura, Grotesque and Xavier Sans; typical serif typefaces include Baskerville, Cheltenham, Galliard and Novarese.

ANNA

Bernard Fashion

COPPERPLATE

Dauphin

Nuptial

Tekton

Shelly Allegro

Zapf Humanist

Some display typefaces include Anna, Bernhard Fashion, Copperplate, Dauphin, Nuptial, Tekton, Shelly Allegro and Zapf Humanist.

tion of using display typefaces—that is, more ornamental typefaces that have been designed to be used for smaller amounts of text. These typefaces can range from being a larger or bolder version of text type to outrageously decorative or hand-drawn typefaces. Calligraphy, antique letters or handlettering can also be used in the same way as these display typefaces.

Choosing a type to use for a letterhead can be a very simple process. Most word processing programs include some form of Times Roman and Helvetica; these have become the standard serif and sans serif typefaces due to their classic design and readability. If these were the only two typefaces you had to work with, you could still design an interesting letterhead by experimenting with type placement, color or paper choice. But chances are you have much more at your disposal, and your type choices are far from limited. So where do you begin?

If a logo already exists, the type should complement the character of the logo. It doesn't have to "match." In fact, the design dynamic can be far more interesting if the type complements and enhances the graphic. If your logo is a name that is in a fancy script, for instance, then a simple sans serif might complement that logo beautifully, whereas the choice of another script would just clutter up your graphic message. And a simple, traditional logo might sparkle when paired with a type that's a little more unexpected.

After you've picked a typeface, your job as a designer is not over; proper setting of the type you've picked is an art that more and more

Color Basics

Color is more than a personal preference—it's also a great graphic tool that must be appropriate to the business or person it's representing. Law firms still prefer the classic engraved letterhead on fine white paper, while most other businesses stick to sedate colors of ink—black and brown, or deep reds, blues or greens—on either white or cream stock. Personal stationery, however, can employ more innovative colors and color combinations. And a business of an artistic nature demands even more creative solutions, both in design and in color. Chapter six has more information about the process and the relative costs of printing in color. But as a general rule, keep in mind that the more colors you use, the more expensive your print job will be.

The most basic color scenario, of course, is the use of a single ink color and one paper color. If you decide on a one-color letterhead, there are very good reasons for using black and white: It's basic, fashionable, cheap, and it need not be boring. It can be printed from any computer, and, if given an interesting design, it can look clean and crisp, strong and important. Remember, too, that there are many different "colors" of white, from warm whites and cream colors to bright bluish whites, and there are also different shades of black (having overtones of blue or brown), so there is some room for tonal variation even within this very basic color scheme.

If you want to use a color of ink other than black, the color needs to be strong enough to "read" easily. A single, deep color on a lighter color of paper—for instance, deep rose on cream—is an effective choice. Other dark colors—such as blue/black, dark brown or maroon—may cost as little as black ink but can give your letterhead a more distinctive look, especially in combination with an unexpectedly complementary color of paper. Another option for stretching this one color is using screen tints—that is, having the printer break up solid areas of color into dots, making lighter values of the color. For example, a dark blue ink combined with a 30 percent tint of the blue for graphic areas and printed on a rose-colored paper will provide more visual interest to your piece than would the use of 100 percent ink alone.

One technique that costs little more than the price of one ink is split-fountain printing; with this technique, two or more colors are printed from one ink fountain that has been divided into two parts, giving you two colors for little more than the price of one ink. Rainbow-fountain printing, in which two inks are printed from one fountain without a divider, provides even greater color variations, as this technique allows the two ink colors to mix in the middle, resulting in a wide array of shades.

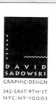

This stationery system designed by David Sadowski, New York, shows how interesting graphics and layout can make a simple black-and-white design effective. Reversing geometric borders and a typeface with a modern feel out of a black rectangle gives this system a fresh look; the black rule on the left is a small touch that keeps the letterhead from looking too stark.

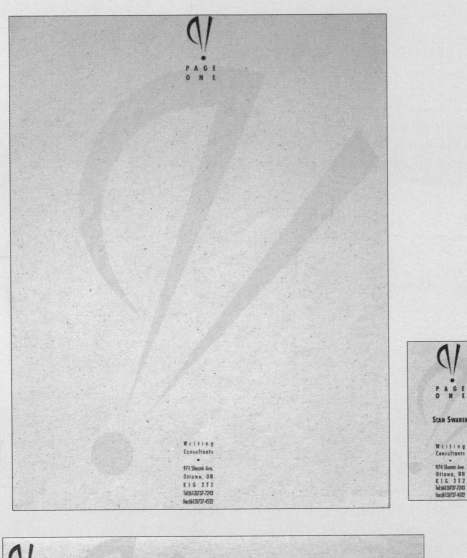

A striking logo and type treatment on tan recycled paper give this one-color stationery system visual interest. A very subtle tinted varnish of the logo is printed large on both the first and second letterhead sheets, as well as on the card and envelope. Design by Terry Laurenzio, 246 Fifth Design Inc., Ottawa, Canada.

Variations for one color:

- Use a gradated blend of a color (from dark to light) for a border.

- Print an area of the paper, not the type, with a bright or dark ink, leaving readable areas of white for the name and address.

- Print the back of your paper with patterns or words in the ink you've chosen—it will show through to the front of the paper and will combine with the color of the paper to give the effect of a second color.

- Print a white design in a black box, planning to hand-color parts of the white design with markers (the edges will bleed into the black and not show).

- Add more color to your system with paper, using a different paper color for each component but using one color of ink throughout. Or use the same color of paper throughout the system, only changing the color of ink from piece to piece. Either way, you're adding a lot of color while staying within a one-color budget.

Color combinations for one ink color:

- Teal ink on cream paper
- Dark gray ink on rose
- Black on gray
- Dark red on pale green
- Brown on peach
- Metallic ink on white

Color Basics

If you have the option of using two ink colors, there will be a lot more potential for variety than with just one. A standard two-color letterhead treatment might include a red logo and dark blue type on a cream-colored stock; a more innovative treatment might combine a yellow logo with red lettering and white paper printed all over with little yellow dots.

To get ideas for color combinations, look at ink or paper sample books (available through your printer and graphic arts stores). Cut color swatches from magazines, get paint chips from hardware stores, and look at how colors are combined in fabrics or in works of art. Or get a color wheel and combine colors that are complementary—that is, opposite one another on the color wheel. The printer will mix an ink as closely as possible to your specifications, or you can use a color-matching system to specify color.

A third color can sometimes be created from two colors by printing overlapping tints of colors. A 15 percent tint of yellow printed over a 10 percent tint of blue, for example, will make a greenish color.

When picking colors, keep in mind that ink is either transparent or opaque. Opaque inks will completely cover the color of the paper, while transparent inks will blend on the paper, which may or may not be a desirable effect. If you want to overlap two or more inks, you need to know which type of inks you're choosing so you'll know how they will act in combination with one another. It's very easy to get muddy color combinations, so talk to your printer and determine this before speccing a job with elaborate color mixes.

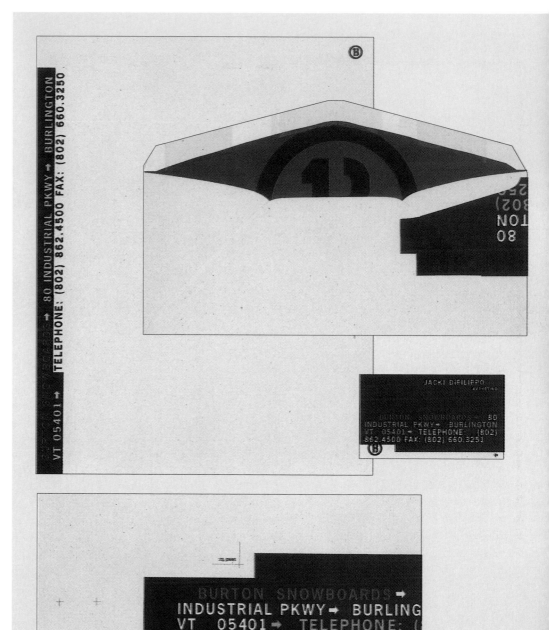

A two-color letterhead designed by Adam Levite of Jager DiPaola Kemp Design in Vermont. The intricate use of black and red on tan paper offers a great deal of graphic variety on the page. Reverses and a tint of gray make this look like more than two colors. Note that the type treatment is kept very simple in contrast and that the inside of the envelope is also printed in red with a large black B logo. The unusual layout on both the letterhead and the envelope is functional yet fresh and contemporary.

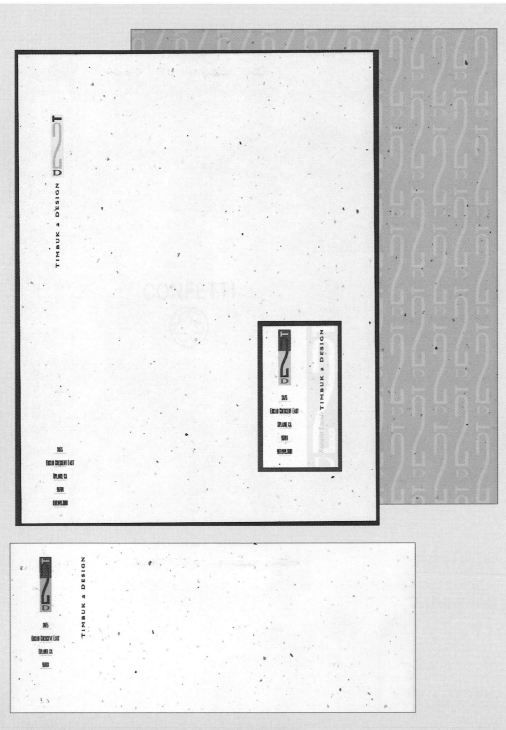

Designer Rossana Lucido used three colors to give her California design firm a striking stationery system. The front is kept subtle, leaving enough room for writing while also showing off the heavily flecked recycled stock. Note that the logo color treatment is different from the letterhead to the business card.

Variations for two colors:

- Use one transparent ink color to cover the entire paper, another opaque color for the type. An unexpected third color will be the parts of the paper that show through the allover transparent ink covering.

- Use the second color just for the rules, ornaments or borders.

- Print a duotone (one color of a dot screen printed over another but slightly offset). This technique is most often used with photographs, but it can look unexpected as a graphic element for its own sake.

- Print a background icon, or other elements, as a screen of one of your inks to create the feel of a third color.

- Double-bump one ink color—that is, print one design in one bright or dark color twice to give it extra vibrancy. This will cost the same as using two ink colors, but the extra impact may be worth it.

Color combinations for two ink colors:

- Red and black ink on bright white paper

- Green and gold metallic ink on cream

- Maroon and forest green on cream

- Pale yellow and red on warm white

- Gold and black on bright white

- Red and dark gray on light gray

Color Basics

Using three or four (or more) matching ink colors is luxurious; design-wise, anything goes just as long as it is printable and affordable. One- and two-color work is usually printed on a one- or two-color press—a process suitable for type, line graphics, or black-and-white halftones. The more passes through the press a printer must do, the more expensive the job will be. Three and four match colors are usually printed on a four- (or more) color press and therefore may cost little more than a two-color job, as both of them will go through the press once.

The use of four match colors is not to be confused with four-color process printing. This more expensive process involves separating an image into dots of the three primary colors (magenta, cyan and yellow) and black. An individual printing plate is made for each color, and the resulting transparent layers of printed dots optically mix on the paper to form the color image. If you are using four-color process printing, your design choices are almost unlimited. You can use photographs, transparencies, paintings, or multiple flat colors and tints. However, it still may not be possible to achieve specific shades you want, especially for fluorescent tints and, of course, metallics; therefore, some designers combine a four-color process design with one or more match colors, using a total of five or more ink colors—a great option, if you can afford it and if you have a design that justifies its use.

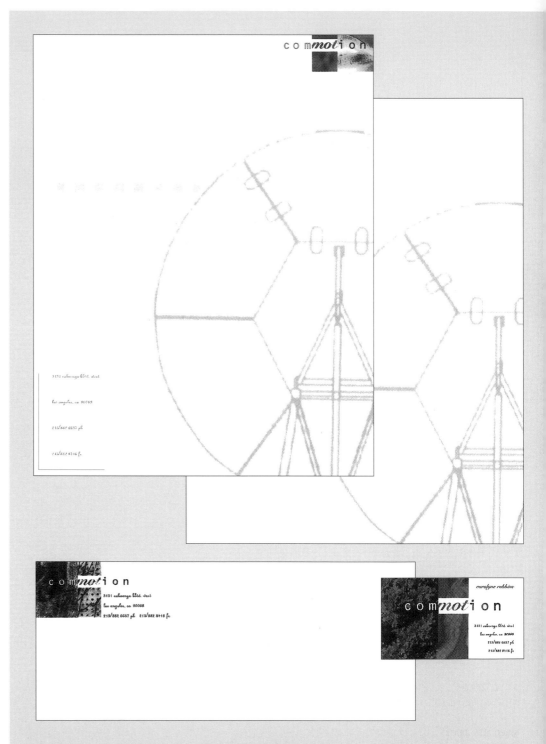

Each piece in this complex system printed by four-color process is unique. Designer Flavio Kampah merges various color images with a type treatment that both reverses out from and overprints the photographs. The images are different on the letterhead, card and envelope, and the type treatment is also varied somewhat. The result is a system that lives up to the name of the California design firm, Commotion.

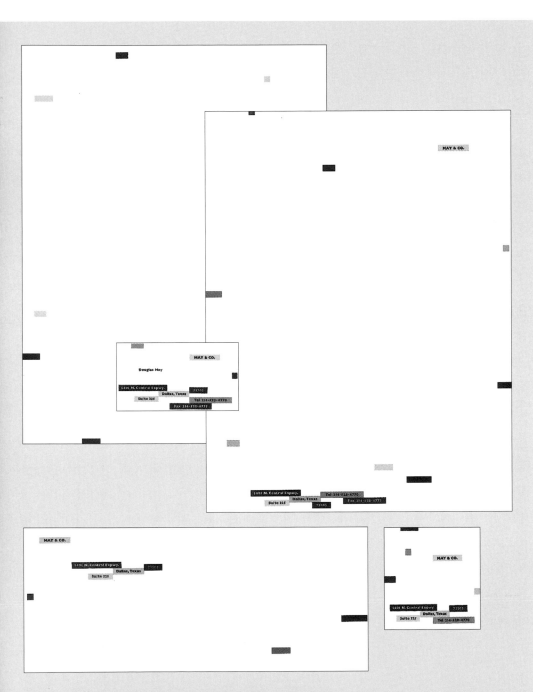

Color combinations for three ink colors:

- Teal, raspberry and gray ink on pale yellow

- Rose, green and black on warm white

- Lime green, fuchsia and black on bright white

- Brown, green and gray on recycled white

- Purple, gold and black on bright white

- Dark blue, maroon and opaque white on pale gray

Color combinations for four ink colors:

- Gold, bright blue, red and black ink on bright white

- Brown, green, rust and black on beige

- Pale tints of red, blue, yellow and black on creamy white

- Black, silver, copper and blue on white

- Purple, mustard, bright pink and dark brown on kraft paper

- Deep green, rose, dark gray and opaque white on pale green

When May & Co. relocated, new business correspondence was created by designers Douglas May and Jo Ortiz. Using a myriad of pure, bright colors on a white background, they were able to reflect the company's energetic approach to design, as well as communicating their informal, interactive office structure. To make the pieces functional, the color blocks are strategically aligned, indicating where to type or fold, and the second sheet is arranged so it can be used in any direction, creating a more diverse presentation when needed.

Special Effects

There are many printing effects that can add interest or style to your letterhead or, in fact, to any component of the system you're designing. Most printers can provide any of these services, although special techniques are laborious and may be quite expensive.

Bleeding color or type off the edge of the paper requires a print area that extends slightly beyond the crop marks and is later trimmed away. It is a great effect for borders, patterns or other types of artwork.

Engraving used to be a standard way of producing a card or letterhead; today it is an expensive (and therefore little-used) form of printing that can lend an air of elegance and selectivity to your project. Engraving is done by carving or etching the letters or image into a metal plate, either by hand, machine or a photo process. The plate is covered with ink, then the surface wiped until only the engraved parts still hold the ink. Finally, the paper is pressed into the plate, creating printed results that are very clean, crisp and detailed. The sharp lines of an engraving are actually inked impressions in the paper, making the letters slightly dimensional, which can be both seen and felt with the hand. However, since details of the art you provide to the engraver are rendered so sharply in the final result, you need to make sure that the art you provide is very precise, as small slipups could be apparent in your final print job. An engraving die is expensive but can be used over and over again; so if you plan to use an engraving of the same element for your entire stationery system, plan to use that element at the same size on every piece.

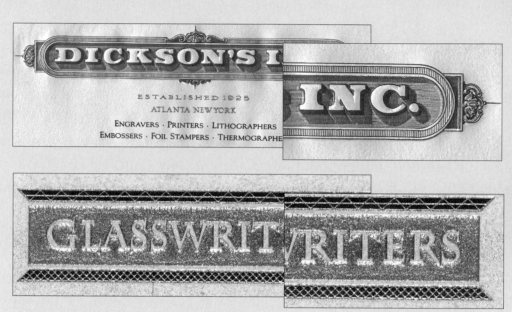

Engraving: These details show how an engraved image makes an actual impression in the paper surface: The letters (or image) are actually raised.

Thermography: These details show how thermography can be used to produce raised lettering or solid background areas. Thermography works best for relatively small areas, such as the black background area of the Get Set logo at top. Note that a (possibly undesirable) texture may be produced over larger areas when using this method.

Thermography is a method of producing raised lettering at much less cost than engraving. The paper is first printed with a slow-drying ink. The ink is then dusted with a resin that sticks to the still wet surface and is then reheated. The resin melts and fuses to the ink, making the area raised. Both fine details and large areas don't respond well to thermography—fine lines get too thick or lumpy, and large areas can develop an orange-peel texture. While thermography doesn't really look or feel like engraving, it can still be an adventurous texture if used for its own sake.

Embossing is similar to engraving, but it creates a more dimensional relief. It also uses a carved metal plate to stretch the paper, creating a three-dimensional image in its surface. It is a lovely technique to use for logos or artwork. Embossing can be inked or left plain (otherwise known as "blind embossing"); in either case, it invites touch. Embossing can also be multi-leveled, creating a real bas-relief. Debossing is the opposite of embossing, creating a lowered impression in the paper surface.

Hot stamping is a form of embossing that uses colored foil rather than ink. Foils come in many metallic colors and textures, even in pearlized colors. The process is hard to control, and color may not prove stable, but it can give a distinctive and deluxe look to your letterhead.

Metallic inks also provide richness and shine, and they come in a range of gold, silver and copper colors made from actual metal particles suspended in the ink. New developments, such as adding metallic powders to process colors, make it

Special Effects

possible to simulate thousands of metallic colors as well as to add metallic highlights to photographs.

Varnish is a layer added to give sparkle or gloss to areas of printing (or over the whole piece as protection). Add emphasis to areas of a photograph with varnish or print a logo in varnish over an area of a dark color. Varnish comes glossy, dull or tinted, and its effect can be sharp or subtle. It is shiniest if used on a coated paper stock, but then is better suited to business cards than letterhead, envelopes, or pieces that need to be written on. Spot varnish can be used on areas of graphics to make them "pop out" of a design on uncoated paper.

Die-cutting cuts holes. You provide the shape to be cut out, and a sharp-edged steel die is made that cuts the shape out of the paper or changes the shape (edges) of the paper. You can use a die-cut simply as a decorative element—for instance, devising a stairstep cutout shape for the corners of a letterhead just because you like the way it looks and it complements the rest of your design. Or you can use a die-cut conceptually, to play on your own or your client's business or name—for example, die-cutting a bite mark in the corner of a dentist's letterhead.

Incorporating any of these special effects requires some extra planning. First, you'll need to make sure any paper you choose is compatible with the process you want to use—lighter weights of paper, for instance, won't be able to stand up to most of these processes. You also need to be aware that these special effects cannot be done in just any order. Processes that make an impression on the paper,

Embossing: The ampersand in the logo for Line & Tone, a service bureau in New York City, is blind embossed. Since blind embossing always appears smaller once printed, the oversized ampersand works in a way that a printed version could not.

such as embossing or engraving, will need to be done last so they won't be flattened by other printing equipment; thermography and foil stamping must also be done last because these elements may melt when stationery bearing them is run through printing equipment. Some combinations of these processes may not be possible, so ask your printer early on before you get your heart set on something that can't be done; if this happens, your printer may be able to suggest acceptable substitutes—for example, metallic ink for foil stamping—or you may have to redesign your piece.

Remember, too, that some effects make it more difficult to use the product. You can't run embossed, foil-stamped or thermographed paper through a laser printer or photocopier because of the heat and pressure, and some die-cuts on the paper edge may cause a printer or photocopier to jam, so keep the end use of the system in mind when incorporating these effects.

And apart from these practical issues, it is important to remember, with any special printing effect, not to get carried away; effects can quickly become overdone or look dated or tired. Any effect you choose should be used as a way to enhance your design—not as a gimmick that is used to hide the lack of a good design.

Foil stamping: This is an interesting example of the use of foil stamping on a textured paper, as the striped surface shows up even more in the foiled areas. The use of reverse type also makes this stationery system look much more elaborate than its actual use of one foil color and one ink color. Design by Image Consultants Advertising, Elmira, New York.

Special Effects

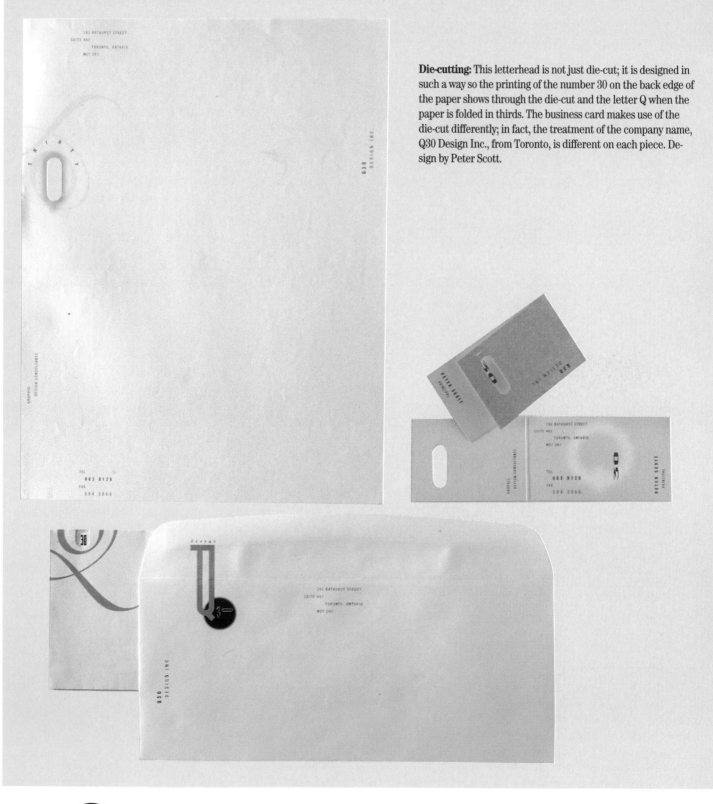

Die-cutting: This letterhead is not just die-cut; it is designed in such a way so the printing of the number 30 on the back edge of the paper shows through the die-cut and the letter Q when the paper is folded in thirds. The business card makes use of the die-cut differently; in fact, the treatment of the company name, Q30 Design Inc., from Toronto, is different on each piece. Design by Peter Scott.

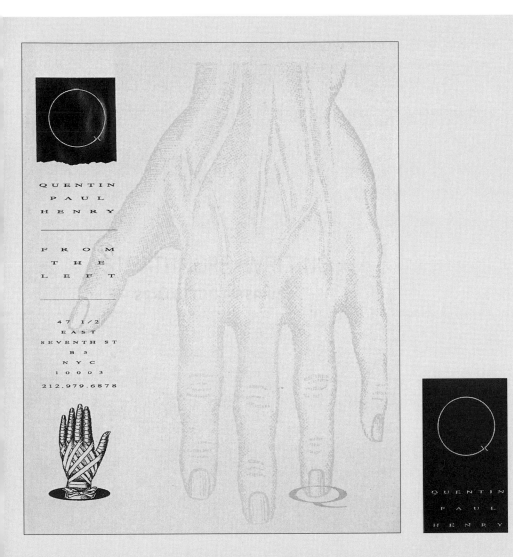

- Die-cut rounded corners on a piece of stationery.

- Double-bump the color of a logo, then cover the area with a glossy varnish.

- Die-cut part of a graphic, then blind emboss the rest.

- Blind emboss a logo that is printed elsewhere on the piece.

- Die-cut the letters of an initial logo.

- Print the background in a metallic color rather than the word or logo.

Stamping: Stamping takes a subtle but important backseat to design in this intricate system by Quentin Paul Henry, New York illustrator and designer. The *Q* is reverse stamped in black on the letterhead. The card, on the other hand, uses the same *Q* stamped in copper on a black field

Graphic Elements

There are many decorative and useful items that can be added to your letterhead in addition to the copy and the logo. These include rules, boxes, borders, ornaments, line art and halftones.

Boxes, rules and other graphic elements are not just decorative items—they can also keep your letterhead page organized. Placing type in a box contains it on the page; colored or screened boxes can run down the side of a letterhead page to set off a list of names, such as a board of directors. Rules can emphasize and separate pieces of information—for instance, a rule above or below the address line will neatly divide the copy from the typed or handwritten areas.

Small lines, boxes or rules can also serve as markers indicating where to place the date, name and address, body of the letter and signature, or where to fold the page after you've written your letter—thus ensuring the visual consistency of communications sent out by a company. These markers can be a fun way to provide a map for using your letterhead.

There are also numerous geometric shapes, decorative symbols or ornaments available that can add interest to stationery. Zapf provides a typeface of interesting and useful dingbats including circles, squares, triangles, arrows, stars and leaves. They can be used along with your type or used alone in any size to create a fancy border, an overall pattern, or as markers for text placement.

Ornaments are fancier than dingbats, more like little pieces of artwork. They have traditionally been used in books to separate chapters or

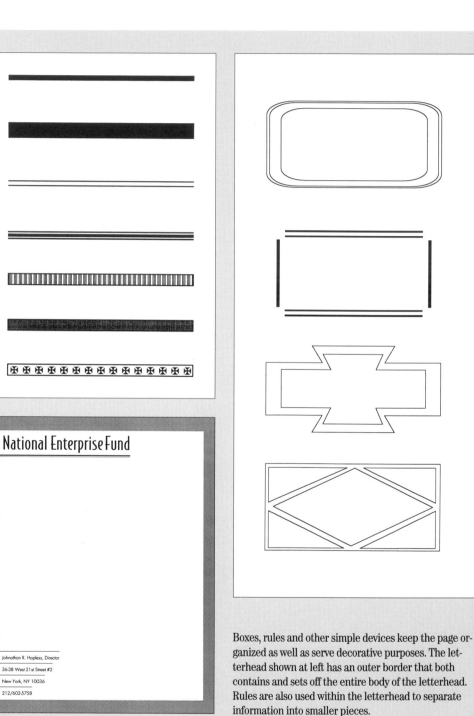

National Enterprise Fund

Johnathan R. Hapless, Director
36-38 West 21st Street #2
New York, NY 10036
212/602-5758

Boxes, rules and other simple devices keep the page organized as well as serve decorative purposes. The letterhead shown at left has an outer border that both contains and sets off the entire body of the letterhead. Rules are also used within the letterhead to separate information into smaller pieces.

Dingbats (top two rows) are available as actual typefaces and can be used within the type or as separate or repeated elements; ornaments (middle two rows) are a bit fancier and can be used like dingbats or combined into borders or rules; clip art (bottom two rows) provides all sorts of small illustrative material.

areas. More recently, however, illustrators and type designers have jumped on this bandwagon, and now dingbats and ornaments are available in numerous styles, such as Celtic or Art Deco, and effects, such as woodcuts. They can be used in the same ways as dingbats.

Rubber stamps are a very inexpensive way to add color and graphic interest to a letterhead system. A stamp can be made from any line art or from type, although it can be difficult to work with a large stamp (ink coverage can get spotty). Ink pads come in a wide variety of wonderful colors, including some that use more than one ink on the pad, giving you a rainbow effect. Whether used for a logo or type, a rubber stamp conveys a casual, playful tone. Rubber stamps are ideal for someone who moves around a lot; all of the information can be printed on the system except for the address, which can be stamped on (and is thus cheap to change).

Illustrations can be commissioned from artists working in painterly techniques, drawings, photographs or on the computer. Calligraphy and hand-lettering can also be commissioned. Computer effects or artwork that may not be available to you can be purchased through design studios or sometimes through service bureaus or printers.

Clip art books—books of copyright-free illustrations—are also widely available. There are also many clip art selections available for the computer; they can be used as part of a logo or as a small graphic accent on a letterhead. Illustrations can also be greatly enlarged and printed as a screen tint on the center of the let-

Graphic Elements

terhead, which can give an effect similar to that of a watermark on your paper. These illustrations can be scanned and used as graphics on the computer. Gray-scale scanners can scan either line art or halftones and can manipulate the image in terms of size and contrast. The images are saved as graphic files to be imported into a page layout or drawing program. Color scanners can import color images into a photo manipulation program, where the images can be changed as much as desired, then imported as graphics. These illustrations usually take up a great deal of computer memory, however, and the images or files are often very large and subsequently given to the printer on disk.

Halftones are another very flexible way to add interest to letterhead design. For a very simple treatment, they can be used as an abstract sort of border. For something more complex, an entire halftone can cover the back of a letterhead, with part of the whole used as a spot decoration on the front of the first page and on the other components.

Remember that any illustration or photograph needs to be either copyright free to begin with or the rights to use the image must be purchased from the photographer, illustrator, or whomever holds the copyright. A stock-photo company will sell you the right to the one-time use of a photograph—the selections are usually vast, from black-and-white historic photos to high-tech color images of people, places and situations.

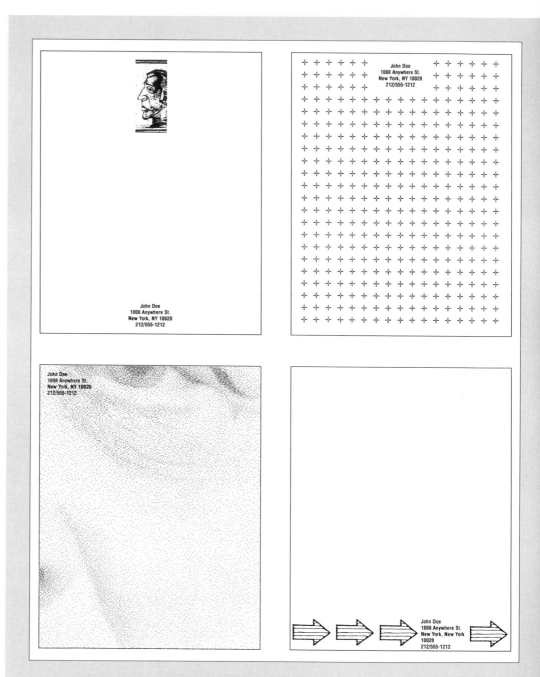

Almost any kind of graphic element can be incorporated into a letterhead. For example, you could use an illustration, an allover background pattern, a screened photograph used as a background, or a decorative border.

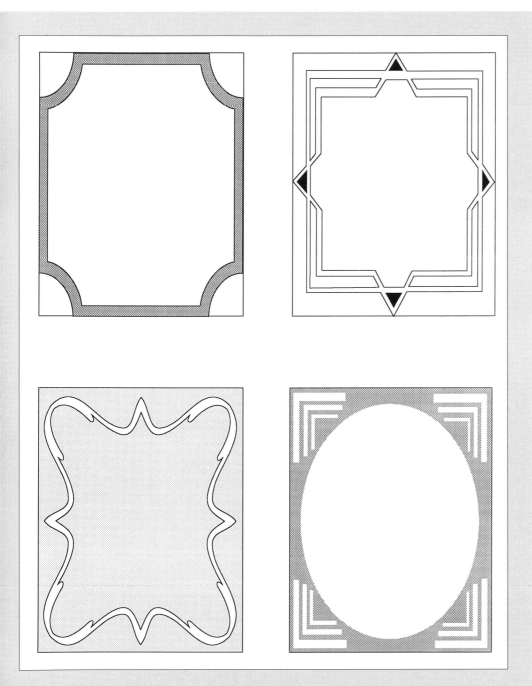

Borders and frames, printed in tints or colors, give a letterhead a sense of containment.

- Use a portion of a map as a graphic element.

- Photocopy a piece of clip art larger and larger until the image breaks up, then reduce it again to get a stamped effect.

- Use a decoration in a different color on each piece of a system.

- Print a large, screened line illustration with a split fountain of ink for more than one color.

- Place a dingbat or a small illustration inside a bold letter to replace, for example, the center of an *O*.

- Repeat rules printed in a second color to make striped paper.

Choosing Paper

There are various ways to see new paper samples. Go to your printer and look through their paper sample books, or write to the paper manufacturers for samples and swatch books. Sending away for paper promotions you see mentioned in ads in graphic design magazines is also a good idea; not only are these beautiful examples of great design, but they often include invaluable production and printing information.

Most paper is available in several weights of book or text stock, several weights of cover or card stock, and in standard-size envelopes. Paper comes coated (a clay coating gives it a glossy surface) and uncoated (available in various textures and finishes).

Traditional letterhead is printed on fine white paper that has a high cotton-rag content (anywhere from 25 to 100 percent), which makes a thin, strong sheet. The impressions and surface textures found in paper have a history in the art of hand-papermaking, where a screen is dipped in a vat of wet paper pulp and pulled up. The screen can be made in ways that leave textures on the paper. Its surface can be laid (you will see thin lines across the surface) or wove (a smoother, woven surface). The finest stocks include a watermark, a logo made of wire that is attached to the papermaking screen, leaving a shallow impression or shadow.

Most letterhead is printed on uncoated paper because it is easier to write on (shiny, coated paper does not take pencil or ink well). The occasional business card uses coated paper, however, and the effect is slick, especially if there are large areas of color. Coated paper also stands up to abuse better than uncoated paper—which is desirable for a business card but irrelevant for stationery. Uncoated paper absorbs ink in the printing process, and the results can be rough or uneven; with coated paper, the ink sits on top of the paper. The smoothness of paper also makes a difference in the printed result—rough or textured paper can cause printing problems with fine areas of type or halftones. The other thing to consider is opacity—you can see through some papers and not through others. You might want a translucent sheet if you are printing on the back side of the paper and want the printing to show through to the front; on the other hand, if you're planning a large colored area, you'll probably want a fairly opaque stock to avoid a distracting image showing through.

Paper also comes in various weights; the basis weight of a particular stock indicates the poundage of five hundred standard-size sheets. The higher the basis weight, the heavier the stock. Bond-paper weights range from 15 to 40 pound, book papers from 30 to 120 pound, and cover stock from 50 to 120 pound. Choose the appropriate weight for the job; a letterhead needs to be strong enough to write on (the standard is 20 to 28 pound), while business cards need to be even sturdier than that.

As concern for the environ-

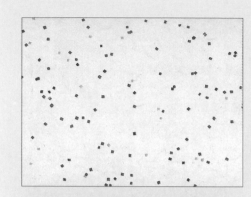

Fancy papers include confetti, graduated tone, marbleized and gray recycled.

ment has grown, recycled papers have become very popular. As suggested by the name, these are papers made from old paper, and they contain flecks and bits of color. Vellum (translucent) paper has also gained in popularity, especially for business cards. It can be used for letterhead, but it is harder to print on and write on and can be quite expensive.

Talk to your printer before you choose paper for a job—small printers, for example, have a very limited number of papers that they regularly stock and won't order special papers unless the job is large enough to use the minimum amount, usually a whole carton of paper.

There are also catalogs for ordering small amounts of specialty papers that can either be run through a laser printer or given to a commercial printer to use. One such catalog is PaperDirect (call (800) A-PAPERS); another is Idea Art (call (800) 433-2278). These catalogs specialize in preprinted, four-color letterhead, brochures and cards meant for computer use, but they also have plain sheets of laser, rag and recycled papers.

If you can, look at samples of your paper choice that have been printed to see the results. It's ideal to test your design on the intended paper, at least by running a sample sheet through the computer in black and white or in color through a service bureau. Pretest its use as well, running it through the equipment it will eventually be run through.

Using a variety of papers gives a unique look to this stationery system by California designer/illustrator Hajdeja Ehline. The letterhead is printed with black type and a green halftone on thin vellum. Since the return address for the envelope has been printed in red, white and black on an adhesive label, various colors and stocks of envelope paper can be used with the stationery. The business card is printed with a blue halftone on heavier vellum—a more practical choice of paper than the lightweight vellum of the letterhead would have been.

Envelopes

The envelope used in most business stationery systems is a #10 (4⅛" x 9½"); however, they come in many other sizes, from a #6 (3⅝" x 8⅜") to a #14 (5" x 11½"). There are also many other shapes of envelopes that can be ordered in white bond, kraft or, sometimes, specialty papers. The envelope should accommodate the folded and printed piece by at least ⅛" all around. Keep postal regulations in mind, particularly when getting envelopes custom made. The minimum mailable size is 3½" in height by 5" in width; the maximum—before postage is increased—is 6⅛" in height by 11½" in width.

Check with your printer to make sure a suitable envelope is available in the paper of your choice. If not, you may have to use an envelope in a different paper stock. It is standard to have the same weight and color of paper for the letterhead and envelope. If you must choose an envelope produced by another paper manufacturer, try to compare the tints closely—and under fluorescent light (the light under which they'll probably be seen)—to make sure they really match. A cream color in one paper is probably not the same as a cream in another. If you can't get a good match, it's preferable to have something that purposely contrasts with the letterhead in color or texture—a pale gray letterhead with a darker gray envelope, for example. A less traditional solution, but especially good for a stationery system that is printed on the back, is the use of a translucent vellum envelope to show off this visual element; what this solution lacks in practicality it makes up for in visual appeal.

If you can't get an envelope in the

In the left-hand column are traditional envelope layouts for type placement; the right-hand column shows some more unusual variations.

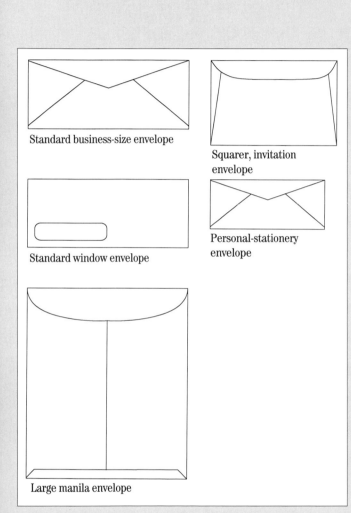

Envelope shapes can be as varied as is necessary to do their two-part job—they must be large enough to contain your written material, and they must conform to postal regulations. Illustrated above are some of the standard shapes.

Standard business-size envelope

Squarer, invitation envelope

Standard window envelope

Personal-stationery envelope

Large manila envelope

size or paper stock you want, consider envelope conversion—printing the paper stock prior to gluing to create a custom envelope. This is an expensive process, but it is also the only way to achieve a number of special effects. For example, it's necessary if you want to have the interior of the envelope printed. It's also the only way to engrave, foil stamp or emboss an envelope on one side only, since any of these processes would affect both sides of the envelope if it were already folded or glued.

Envelope layout has more possibilities for creativity than you might expect; it's not necessary to stick to the usual upper left-hand corner or back flap for placing the copy. First consider what is important to include on the envelope. At minimum, you want the address and zip code. More often, the envelope will mimic the design and elements of the letterhead. This might include a logo and the company or person's name as well as the address.

Most copy is placed somewhere on the left-hand side of the envelope, leaving the right side for the stamp and address. This is practical, and the post office is used to it. While there is an art form of hand-decorating postcards or envelopes, the results can be creative but confusing. For printing, however, and especially for a business, there should be a balance of the creative and the practical.

As for color, you'll generally want to match the color of the envelope to the paper, but if you

choose the color to contrast with or complement the letterhead, there are some practical issues to consider. If you go with an envelope that's lighter in color than the letterhead, there's a chance the letterhead will show through the envelope, so you might consider choosing a heavier weight of paper. If you choose an envelope that's darker than your letterhead—or if you choose any brightly colored envelope that's a different color from your letterhead—the color of the envelope could run onto the letterhead if the envelope gets wet. You might think that this is an unlikely occurrence, but if you have a machine that moistens and seals all your correspondence, it isn't. As always, pretest your choice before you commit to a large print run.

There are pluses and minuses to designing a system with an odd-size envelope: It can get attention and could give you a better canvas for a creative layout; but consider that a nonstandard-size envelope, especially a larger one, is more likely to be mangled by post office equipment and that it might also cost more to mail.

Some businesses require more than one type of envelope; there might be a variant with a clear panel that the company uses to send out invoices or a business-reply envelope that it encloses in direct-mail pieces or other correspondence requiring a quick response. Consider using a grid to ensure consistency in all the envelopes you design for the same company.

Labels & Other Pieces

There are other printed pieces that often go along with a stationery system. These include second sheets, labels, folders or binders, notepaper, postcards and response cards.

Second sheets of letterhead (the sheet that is used for the second page of a letter) are often-overlooked opportunities for creativity. While second sheets often consist of the same stock as the original piece, unprinted, you can use a different weight or even a different stock of paper. For example, you could print a tinted version of the logo in a corner or large all over the page. Or you could print the back of the second sheet or use a die-cut on the letterhead so a printed element on the second sheet shows through to the top sheet. Or consider carrying over a graphic element used on the first page to the second page—for instance, if you were designing a system for a marathon event and had a footprint border at the bottom of the first sheet, you could continue the footprints to the second sheet. Of course, details such as these will cost more than just going with an unprinted sheet of paper, but the attention to detail you're showing by dreaming up such clever graphic elements will undoubtedly impress recipients.

Notepaper (which is usually a bit smaller than letterhead and folded in half to fit in a squarish envelope) is often needed in situations when a warmer, handwritten message is appropriate, such as thank-you notes.

Mailing labels should be consistent with the letterhead design, even though they are likely to be printed using a different paper stock (the usual labels are either paper-gummed or crack-and-peel, which

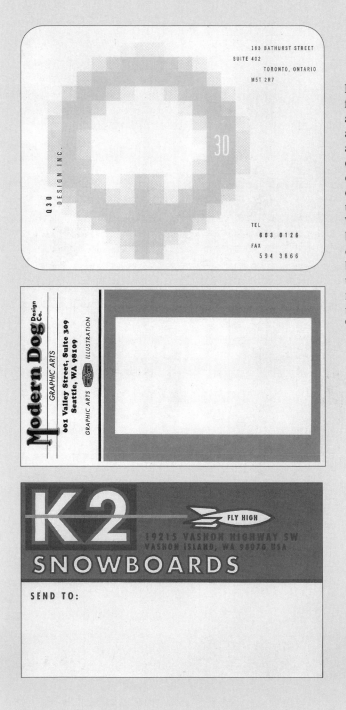

Labels: Top, a paper-gummed label, from Q30 Design, in which the unusual layout works because the graphic is a light color that can be printed over as needed. Designer: Peter Scott. Middle, a crack-and-peel label from Modern Dog Graphics. Note how the label echoes the rest of the letterhead system, shown on page 107. Designers: Vittorio Costarella, Michael Strassburger, Robynne Raye. Bottom, a crack-and-peel label from K2 Snowboards. This label has a more traditional layout, with the company's name and address running across the top of the label. Designers: Brent Turner, Vittorio Costarella.

COYOTE MOON

*Inspirations in Fine Clothing
and Beyond*

Celebrating our bodies –
with elegance & comfort in
Clothing
Festive Jewelry
Colorful Accessories

Soothing our spirits –
with
Musical Chimes
Incense
Fragrant Candles
Devotional Statues

T-shirts ★ Tapes ★ Cards ★
Unusual Gifts

54 Main Street
Belfast, Maine 04915
207-338-5659

A bookmark given out to customers by
Coyote Moon, a retail store in Maine.
A bookmark is a relatively inexpensive
promotional item that can be quite effective. Designer: Carol Gillette.

A self-promotional brochure used by Studio Wilks. Designer: Teri
Wilks. The colors, the type, the logo, and even the relative placement of
items all match the letterhead as closely as possible. The brochure
measures 2¾" x 8½" when closed, an ideal size to stuff into any standard-size business envelope along with routine correspondence or any
other mailings.

MAY & CO.

A decorative label used by May & Co. (The rest of their stationery system is shown on page 31.) Not a mailing label as such, this "purely decorative" item is one more (colorful) way for the company to add its
name to every package it sends out.

limits your paper choices). You can
use the same typeface, logo and colors as on the letterhead, but the layout may not be the same. Often the
area printed on a label is a space of
about an inch across the top or along
the side, leaving the maximum room
for the name and address. At a minimum, the label should include the
same information as the envelope—
logo, address and zip code. Color will
also be dictated by the letterhead
treatment, although to save money
you might choose a simpler, single-
color treatment. Think about using
colors on the label that coordinate
with or contrast with the envelope
that will receive the label.

Binders and folders are often
printed with a logo or other information and die-cut to hold a business
card. Memo pads are sometimes
printed to go along with a folder for a
presentation. Postcards, response
cards, and promotional items such as
bookmarks are all printable and
might need to fit into your design
scheme. Even invoices and other
business forms need to retain the
company look. Self-mailers need a
heavier stock of paper, but they can
be a very creative way to send a handwritten note. Think of interesting
ways to close a mailer (a wax stamp,
a die-cut and string, gumming or even
Velcro). Be sure, however, that your
planned piece will conform to postal
regulations in both size and finishing
techniques.

Packaging is a whole other area,
but depending on the business, it
may evolve from the design of a simple business card. Logos and other elements often show up on T-shirts,
mugs, pens and even trucks or air-
planes. The lesson is to think ahead.

Project 3: A Simple Design Using

The Client: Tabletop, Inc., is a company that imports items for the tabletop, such as dishes, lamps, vases, candlesticks and cutlery. The owner came to me with an old logo and stationery system that had been very simple and in just black and white. He wanted, at first, to keep the old logo and simply add some color to the pieces. We agreed that using a table as the *T* in "Tabletop" was a very logical way to make the company name graphic, but I felt the treatment could be redone with more style. The name of the company is descriptive but not specific, so the owner not only wanted a new treatment of the logo and type, but also wanted the letterhead to reflect some of the other products that the company imports. And since the business had grown, it was time to inject some fun and some color into the letterhead.

After some discussion, we came up with the idea of using small, colorful, tabletop-related icons that could change on each printed piece. To begin, we picked a vase, a glass, a lamp and a cup from some clip art files. We also discussed using cutlery, and because the images of a knife and fork are so vertical, I began to think of them not just as visual elements, but also as typographical forms, like slash marks or exclamation points. This idea evolved into using all the icons for positioning areas of type by marking places where the date, address, or the beginning of the letter would go.

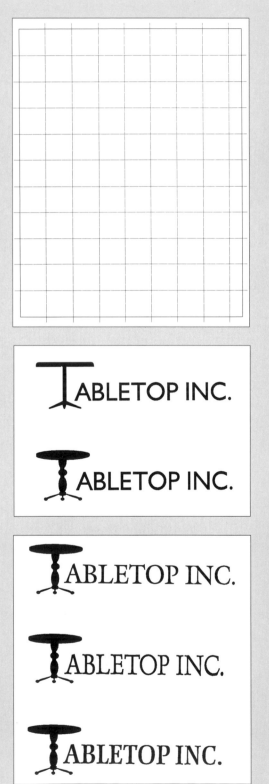

Step 1. For an 8½" x 11" sheet of stationery, I planned a simple grid of 1" x 1" squares. I drew the grid in my drawing program, grouped the lines so they would always stay together, then superimposed the grid on top of my 8½ " x 11" page, starting from the upper left-hand corner (this leaves ½" on the right side due to the paper size). I selected the grid rules and changed the color to a blue tint so the lines would be lightly visible but wouldn't interfere as I placed the type and graphics.

Step 2. The old logo (top) used a table to replace the T in the company name. The owner felt the logo was too hard and industrial looking, and he wanted a softer, more homey approach. I made a new table in my drawing program (second image), essentially combining ovals and circles into the shape I wanted (pictures of pedestal tables in decorating magazines provided my reference material). I filled each element that composed the table with black and again grouped the whole thing. The new table looked out of place combined with the old typeface, so I tried some softer versions of type—(third, fourth and fifth images, respectively) Galliard, Dauphin and Ellington. Consulting with the client, we liked the Dauphin best and proceeded with that typeface.

a Grid

The Assignment: Use a grid to arrange the elements in a letterhead and the other items in a stationery package.

Specifications:

Hardware: PC 386

Software: CorelDRAW

Type:
"Tabletop, Inc.": Dauphin
Address: Gill Sans Condensed

Colors: PMS 476 brown, PMS 186 red and PMS 301 blue

Paper: Three shades of a tan recycled stock

Step 3. Now I wanted to have some fun with the letterhead layout. The other necessary items are the address and phone number, but I had an idea for a date line, so I chose to do that first. A date line needs space for three items—month, day and year—and is often shown by three slanting vertical lines used to separate these items. My idea was to use a knife, spoon and fork instead of the lines. I went to a special type menu in my drawing program that contains small symbols in all sorts of categories. My cutlery appeared as a circled icon (a universal symbol meant to indicate a restaurant). The circle was easy to remove by ungrouping the object, then deleting the circle. I then filled the objects with black and skewed them 20 percent.

Ideas for using a grid to help create letterhead:

- Use a proportional checkerboard grid all over the page.

- Split the page in half, or into quarters, varying the grid in each part.

- Use invisible columns or boxes repeated on the page to contain type and graphics.

- Turn portions of the grid into visible graphic elements that can be used as guides for positioning parts of the letter.

Step 4. To finish the date line, I drew a ½-point line across the width of one of the grid squares and spaced the cutlery across the line. For the address and phone number, I used a simple condensed sans serif face so it would read easily at a small size and make a nice contrast to the more decorative logo face. I picked another tabletop icon to go with the address line, again from my symbol menu. The proportions of the lamp suited the vertical nature of the words it needed to accompany. I placed the address and lamp in a section of the grid in the lower left, making the size of the letters fit nicely in one square. The phone number sits below the square.

Project 3: A Simple Design Using a

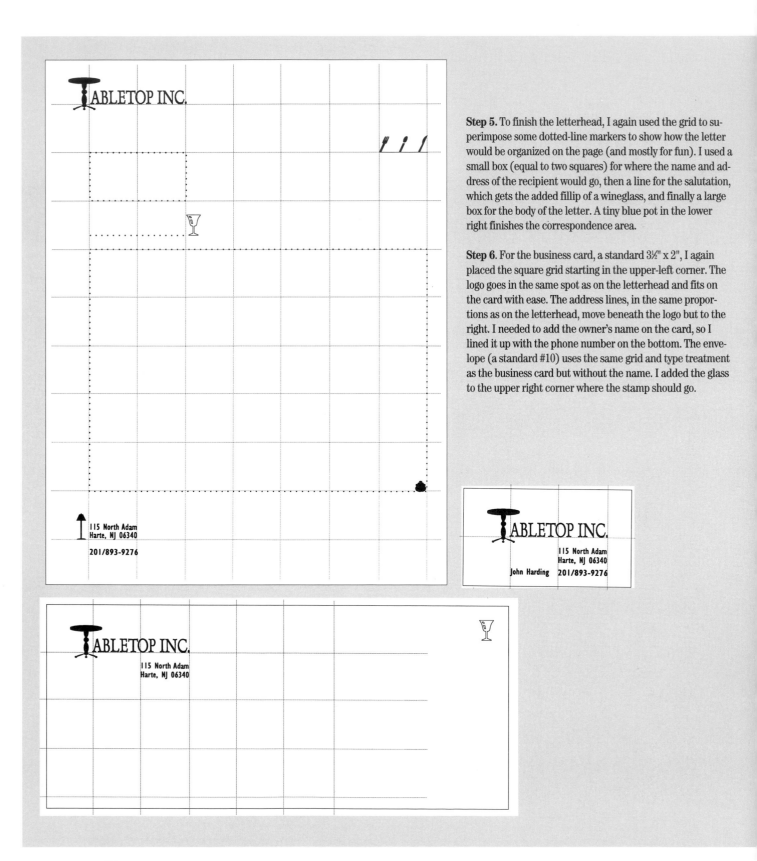

Step 5. To finish the letterhead, I again used the grid to superimpose some dotted-line markers to show how the letter would be organized on the page (and mostly for fun). I used a small box (equal to two squares) for where the name and address of the recipient would go, then a line for the salutation, which gets the added fillip of a wineglass, and finally a large box for the body of the letter. A tiny blue pot in the lower right finishes the correspondence area.

Step 6. For the business card, a standard 3½" x 2", I again placed the square grid starting in the upper-left corner. The logo goes in the same spot as on the letterhead and fits on the card with ease. The address lines, in the same proportions as on the letterhead, move beneath the logo but to the right. I needed to add the owner's name on the card, so I lined it up with the phone number on the bottom. The envelope (a standard #10) uses the same grid and type treatment as the business card but without the name. I added the glass to the upper right corner where the stamp should go.

Grid

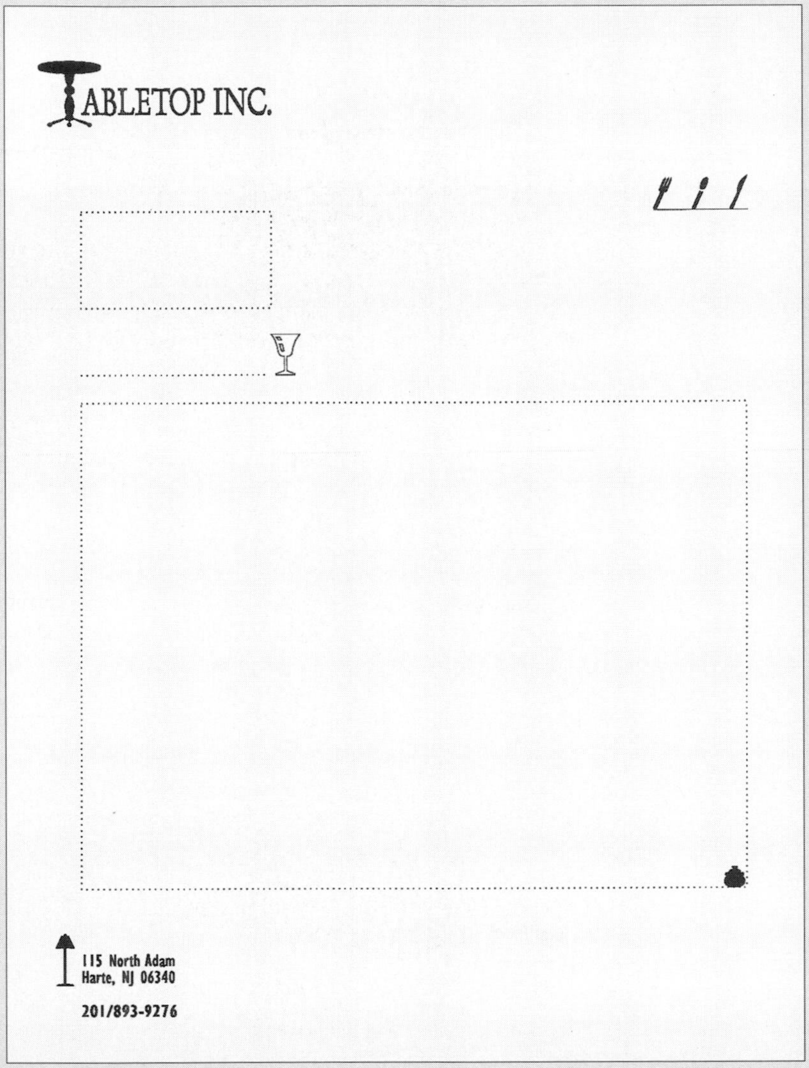

TABLETOP INC.

115 North Adam
Harte, NJ 06340

201/893-9276

TABLETOP INC.

115 North Adam
Harte, NJ 06340

John Harding   201/893-9276

TABLETOP INC.

115 North Adam
Harte, NJ 06340

Step 7. The letterhead is printed on a tan recycled stock. The logo and type are a dark brown, the dotted lines are red, and the icons are a deep blue. The business card and envelope use darker shades of the same paper stock and both of these are simply printed in the dark brown.

Project 4: Quick Letterhead

The Client: Pigtail Publishing evolved from a book the client, Carol Kudeviz, wrote about a little girl and her feelings about the birth of her baby sister. The book is a response to real-life events and is geared to help both parents and children deal with the positive and negative feelings families have when a new child comes into the family.

The proposal was rejected from several mainstream publishers, however, so Carol decided to take a different approach. Her husband owns a printing company, and they decided to manufacture the book themselves. She needed a company name and letterhead so she could begin marketing efforts and turned to her sister, designer Helena Guzzy, for help. The name of the company came from the fact that Carol's daughter has pigtails. Talking on the phone, Carol and Helena came up with the idea of using a drawing of an actual pigtail somewhere in the design. Because the printing was free, Helena could use several colors in the design, but the paper would be whatever white letterhead stock Carol's husband had on hand.

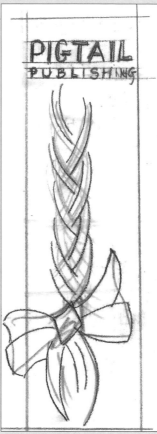

Step 1. The designer began by devising a logo for the company, which would include a type treatment for the name and a drawing of a pigtail. She roughly sketched a couple of pigtails with bows—one straight pigtail and a pair of curved ones—on tissue using colored pencils.

Step 2. Helena showed these sketches to an artist friend and asked him to draw a more finished black-and-white version of each that she could scan and use as art on the computer. She then brought both versions into FreeHand as line art (a TIFF file). She made the straight pigtail brown with a black bow and the curved pigtail blonde with a blue bow. She also made a mirror image of the curved pigtail, so it curved in the opposite direction, to provide more options when combining the pigtail with the type.

Layout

The Assignment: Quickly design a complete stationery system for a new publishing company—to be printed within three weeks.

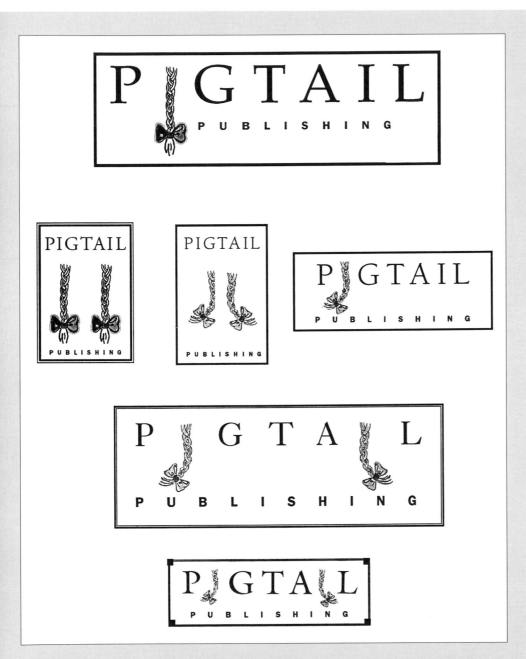

Specifications:

Designer: Helena Guzzy

Pigtail drawings: Rudy Jaimes

Hardware: Macintosh Quadra; Microtek scanner; QMS color printer; Apple IIG printer

Software: Aldus FreeHand, QuarkXPress

Type:
  "Pigtail": Matrix
  "Publishing": Futura
  Address: Century
  Name on business card: Century Bold

Colors: PMS 520 purple and PMS 186 dark red

Paper: Nekoosa Classic Laid white bond

Fast ideas for letterhead designs:

- If you need a logo but don't have much time to create one, consider using an existing photo of the client's house, pet or hand as a ready-made logo.

- Use other ready-made graphics, such as clip art rules, borders, dingbats, and other artwork that can be used "as is" or with minimal manipulation.

- Turn the client's name into a large blind embossing or a die-cut.

- Create ruled paper, like notebook paper, in an offbeat color.

- Consider a simple one- or two-face type treatment—either with or without graphics—and let color provide the punch.

Step 3. The next step was to open a new document in QuarkXPress in order to combine the pigtails with type. She imported the pigtail art by drawing a picture box and using the "get picture" command. Then she made several versions of the logo, trying the pigtail both as a graphic addition to the name and also as a replacement for the letter I. Helena experimented with various typefaces for the name, including Garamond, Berkeley and Century, as well as Matrix (which was actually used). Using Futura for the word "Publishing" provides a nice contrast to the serif face above it. Helen used brown and yellow for the pigtails and a medium blue for the lettering, then printed proofs of the logo on a color printer. She sent these proofs to her sister, who loved the idea of the pigtail used within the name (but just one), but she didn't care for the frame around the logo. She also wanted to use more "unrealistic" colors for the hair, so she chose a purple and a pink to make the concept more fun.

Project 4: Quick Letterhead Layout

Step 4. The next set of sketches played with the pigtail logo in conjunction with the rest of the type on the page. Helena set the address line in Century, spacing the name and address with bullets so the type would go from edge to edge but not be too large. She tried different layouts, placing the logo both centered and flush left. These were faxed to her sister, and a decision was made the same day to use the version in which the pigtail curves right and the logo is centered on the page. Helena then created a final version of the type-and-pigtail combination and saved the QuarkXPress page as an EPS file (PostScript). Since an EPS file can then be brought into a new document and scaled up or down just like any piece of art, this saves time when you need different sizes of a logo for different pieces of printed matter, as Helena would for the envelope and business card.

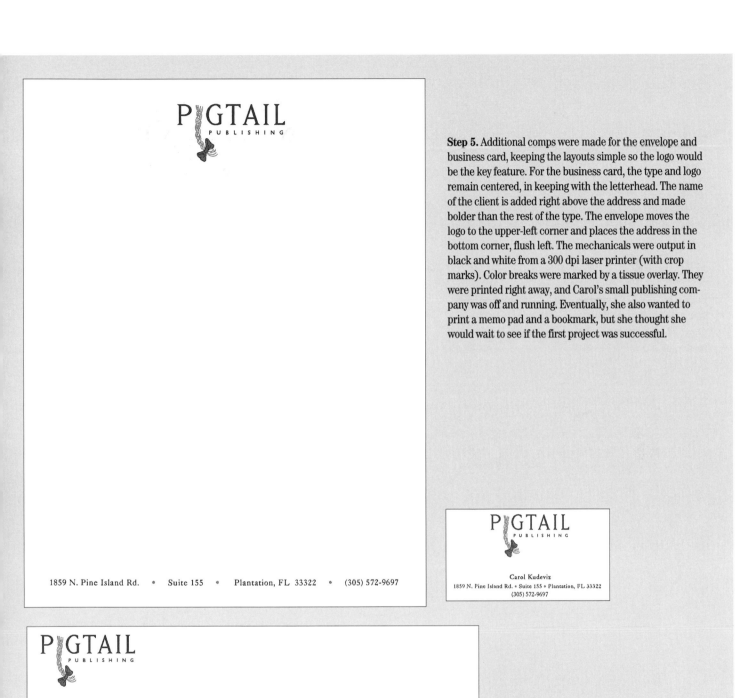

Step 5. Additional comps were made for the envelope and business card, keeping the layouts simple so the logo would be the key feature. For the business card, the type and logo remain centered, in keeping with the letterhead. The name of the client is added right above the address and made bolder than the rest of the type. The envelope moves the logo to the upper-left corner and places the address in the bottom corner, flush left. The mechanicals were output in black and white from a 300 dpi laser printer (with crop marks). Color breaks were marked by a tissue overlay. They were printed right away, and Carol's small publishing company was off and running. Eventually, she also wanted to print a memo pad and a bookmark, but she thought she would wait to see if the first project was successful.

1859 N. Pine Island Rd. • Suite 155 • Plantation, FL 33322 • (305) 572-9697

PIGTAIL
PUBLISHING

Carol Kudeviz
1859 N. Pine Island Rd. • Suite 155 • Plantation, FL 33322
(305) 572-9697

PIGTAIL
PUBLISHING

1859 N. Pine Island Rd. • Suite 155 • Plantation, FL 33322

Project 5: Going From Logo to

The Client: Patricia Smith, the owner of Pink House Design, wanted a letterhead to reflect the flexibility of her design company. While primarily a garden designer, Patricia also provides decorative products for the home, especially interesting antique containers that can hold plants or flowers (silk, dried or real). Her clients are upscale, either permanent or weekend residents of a country community. She wanted her stationery to be encompassing rather than specific to landscape design so if she wanted to use it to promote her interior design products, it would also be suitable. Her business has evolved primarily through word of mouth, so she planned to use the letterhead to do some local self-promotion, using the letterhead to make a flyer that could be produced on a photocopier. Eventually, the idea of a brochure to distribute through antique and decorative-gift stores seemed logical.

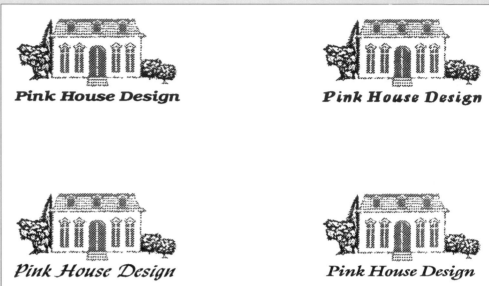

Step 1. First the logo needed type. I wanted to use a typeface that suited the old-fashioned quality of the logo. It could also be a bit feminine, as this is a woman-run company; hence, the italic face. But using a fancy script typeface would have been too elaborate with the image. I experimented with a variety of typefaces, making each one bold: clockwise from top left are Mercurius, Bookman, Galliard and Lydian Cursive. The Galliard Bold Italic seemed to have the right sense of weight combined with movement. I sized the type so the company name was the same width as the illustration. As this is a two-color job, the type is the same dark green (PMS 576) as the bushes.

Step 2. I also wanted to use some graphic interest beyond the logo. I made a small border of leaves using illustrations from the same clip art that I used for the bushes in the logo. I arranged the nine different leaves into a pleasing line, grouped them, colored them green, and saved them as an EPS file to bring into the letterhead.

Letterhead System

Specifications:

Hardware: Macintosh IIci, PC 386, photocopier, HP ScanJet

Software: CorelDRAW, PageMaker

Type:
"Pink House Design," "gardens" and "interiors": Galliard Bold Italic
Remaining text: Galliard

Paper: Nekoosa 80# Natural Opaque Offset

Colors: PMS 576 dark green and PMS 198 pink

Interesting ways to use a logo on letterhead:

- Repeat a logo as a border across the top and bottom of the page.

- Repeat a logo all over the page, changing its colors or tints.

- Use tiny logos to make up a larger image.

- Enlarge the logo to fill (or nearly fill) the entire letterhead page, then screen it back and use it as a background.

- Change the treatment of the logo from letterhead to envelope; for example, use different sizes, colors or placements just to create visual interest.

Step 3. The next step was to experiment with the placement of the logo on the 8½" x 11" page. The logo with the type beneath was a comfortable fit, but I wasn't completely sure how I wanted to balance the page. I first tried the most obvious idea: placing the logo in the upper-left corner of the page. I imported the leaf border art and added the words *gardens* and *interiors* (separated by a bullet) in the same typeface and size as the company name, but all lowercase to give it a bit less importance. The rest of the necessary information sits comfortably beneath in Galliard also, but 10 point and not bold or italic. A second version centers the logo at the top of the page and spreads the border and type across the bottom of the page. In case the client didn't like the border, a third layout places just one leaf between the words *gardens* and *interiors* instead of the bullet.

Project 5: Going From Logo to Letter-

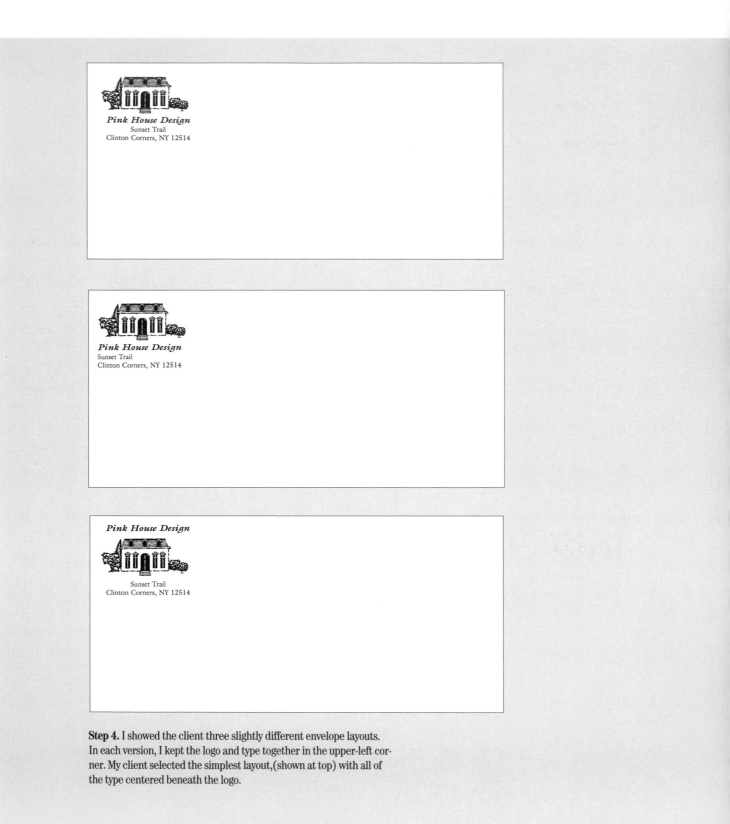

Step 4. I showed the client three slightly different envelope layouts. In each version, I kept the logo and type together in the upper-left corner. My client selected the simplest layout,(shown at top) with all of the type centered beneath the logo.

Pink House Design
Sunset Trail
Clinton Corners NY 12514

Step 5. Here is the finished letterhead and envelope in color. We picked a simple, white paper stock to show off the colors to good advantage. (A business card is created to go along with the rest of the letterhead system in project 10.)

gardens • interiors

Patricia P. Smith

914/266-8492
Fax: 914/373-8911

Pink House Design
Sunset Trail
Clinton Corners NY 12514

Project 6: Designing With Color

The Client: Collins Consulting is a small, conservative consulting company with offices in three cities. They work mainly in the financial sector. Previously, the company was using a plain white letterhead with a simple type treatment and layout, available from any printer. In several ways, this client was typical of many businesses that want new stationery designed: The owner wanted a more interesting image but had no logo and no budget to develop one. He wanted letterhead that was eye-catching but not "artsy." The look had to be broadly appealing, while still indicating such qualities as solidity and trust with just a dash of innovation—all the qualities one would look for in a consulting company. The print quantity would be high (three thousand copies of letterhead, envelope and business cards), so printing in two colors on a good quality sheet of paper was acceptable.

This job was a real design challenge—a client who wanted something to look nice but had no direction and no logo or other graphics, just a name and address. In this situation, it is hard to know where to begin or how to proceed without wasting time or going in directions that won't work out in the end. But it is a scenario that happens more often than not. For this job, I had three factors to go on: a conservative image, a couple of colors and some words. The task was therefore to develop a layout, a color treatment and a type treatment. I began with the colors, asking the client which colors he liked and which colors he envisioned suited his industry. The colors we talked about were traditional, masculine colors: pale gray, teal blue, deep brown, navy blue and burgundy red.

Step 1. I began by thinking about the whole page and how to break up that page using two different colors. The standard treatment would be to use one dark color and one light color on a white or pale-colored paper stock. Two medium shades are also possible, but one color has to be dark enough for the type to be readable. I thought about different color combinations, keeping in mind what the client's preferences were—blue/raspberry, teal/brown, gray/burgundy, forest green/tan, and navy/gray. Then I sketched some layout ideas using these colors with markers on paper.

Creating Logos & Letterheads

The Assignment: Design stationery that uses color as its main feature.

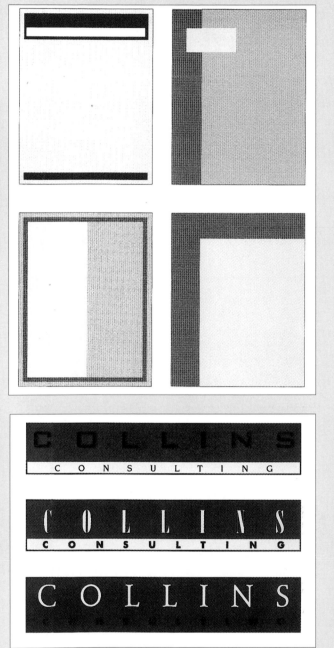

Step 2. Several of the layouts looked like they would work, so I took those ideas to the computer. After making minor modifications, I repeated the four designs I liked best as small images on the page, applied the appropriate PMS colors, and took the page to a service bureau for color output. I showed this page to the client, and his immediate preference was the gray and burgundy sketch at the top left.

Step 3. Now I needed a type treatment to go with my layout. The sheet of paper would be white but printed with a tint of a dark gray that would bleed off the page on all four sides (leaving white only for the type areas). The white boxes with red borders would both contain and set off the type. I didn't want the red to be so dark that I couldn't overprint, nor so light that I couldn't drop out type. I began with the larger red box, exploring several ways to use type within that format.

Specifications:

Hardware: PC 386

Software: CorelDRAW; Aldus Page-Maker

Type:
"Collins": Onyx
"Consulting" and other information: Futura

Colors: PMS 400 gray and PMS 193 burgundy

Paper: White classic laid

Project 6: Designing With Color

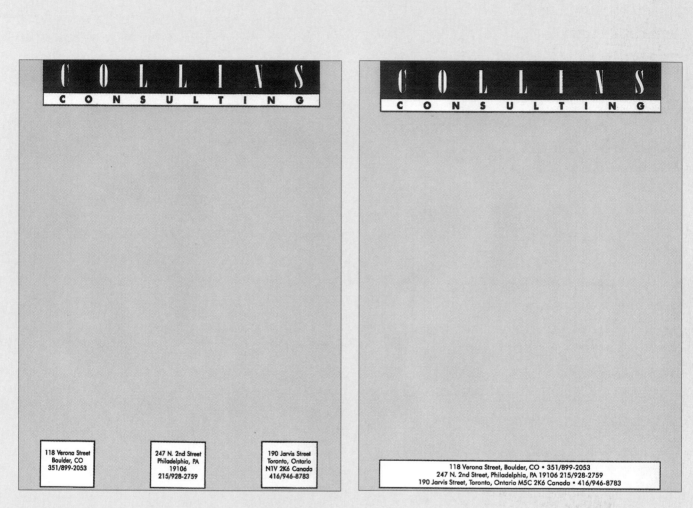

Step 4. Using addresses for all three locations, I next showed the client two different ways to treat the address type at the bottom of the page, again set off in white boxes with red rules.

118 Verona Street, Boulder, CO • 351/899-2053
247 N. 2nd Street, Philadelphia, PA 19106 215/928-2759
190 Jarvis Street, Toronto, Ontario M5C 2K6 Canada • 416/946-8783

Step 5. The final letterhead, envelope and business card are both conservative and colorful. The envelope repeats the letterhead design, but uses an area of gray that goes a third of the way across the envelope. The card is all gray, but the address surprints. The colors shown on these final comps are a little different than the ones that were eventually to be printed. (The cards use just one address as they are provided for each person at each location.)

118 Verona Street, Boulder, CO • 351/899-2053

118 Verona Street, Boulder, CO

Project 7: Imaginative Design

The Client: Pink Sky is a film production company moving into new and more artistically challenging areas, and the owners wanted a letterhead treatment that was as creative and interesting as some of their new projects. This meant I had the freedom to be quite artistic with the letterhead—manipulating type and using color and images in any way I thought appropriate.

Previously, they had been using letterhead that was very simple: The words "Pink Sky" were larger and (logically) pink, with the rest of the copy in black, just centered at the bottom of the page. Now they wanted a logo, had a budget for however many colors were necessary, and wanted to play up their unusual name.

This gave me some logical places to begin: the image of sky and the color pink. I immediately thought of using vellum (translucent) paper, as this would accentuate the idea of air and sky. (You can now purchase vellum paper that will work easily with laser printers and photocopiers.) I also wanted to have the name floating somehow in an actual image of a sky. My first step, then, was to go out and take some black-and-white photos of puffy, white clouds. This was fun, and when the film was developed, I had a range of useable images. I picked a detail of one that I thought would be suitable as a background with type overlaid.

Step 1. The first challenge was to make at least one word in the name look as if it were floating. There are many ways to manipulate type with various computer programs. I picked LetraStudio because I knew the program had envelopes that, when applied to type, automatically put the letters in perspective. I chose to set the word *sky* in Bodoni and used a 70-point type so it was easy to see on-screen. Then I applied the envelope shape to put the word in perspective. This gave the word the floating, receding-into-the-distance look I wanted.

Step 2. I made the color of the word sky a shade of blue and added a band of descriptive words (in black) that named some of the things you find in the sky. I curved the words by joining them to an invisible ellipse shape using the "fit text to path" command. This band was superimposed over the large sky letters so it almost appeared to encircle them. The effect was similar to a banner being flown across the sky.

Using Images

The Assignment: Make a unique letterhead for a very creative company.

Step 3. Next I took a photo of a sky full of white clouds (left) and scanned them (bottom left), using the posterizing option in the scanning program to further abstract the image. (The posterizing option provides a screened-back version of the image.) I saved the image as a TIFF file to use later.

Step 4. I opened a new 8½" x 11" page in QuarkXPress, placed a picture box, and imported the photo of the sky. One nice feature about this program is that the box serves as a cropping device for a picture; you can move the image around in the box, but its perimeter will remain the size and shape of the box. To finish the logo, I added the word pink. I wasn't sure at first that I wanted the word to actually be *pink*—it might seem too cute—but setting the word in a blocky typeface (Helvetica Black) and making the pink a strong, vibrant hue proved amusing in contrast to the poetic sky.

Specifications:

Hardware: Macintosh II, Microtek scanner

Software: QuarkXPress, LetraStudio

Type:
    "Sky": Bodoni
    "Pink": Helvetica Black
    "wind and clouds and birds and": Helvetica Bold
    "Pink Sky Productions": Cheltenham
    Address and phone number: Helvetica

Colors: PMS 2995 blue and PMS 219 pink

Paper: Vellum

Project 7: Imaginative Design Using

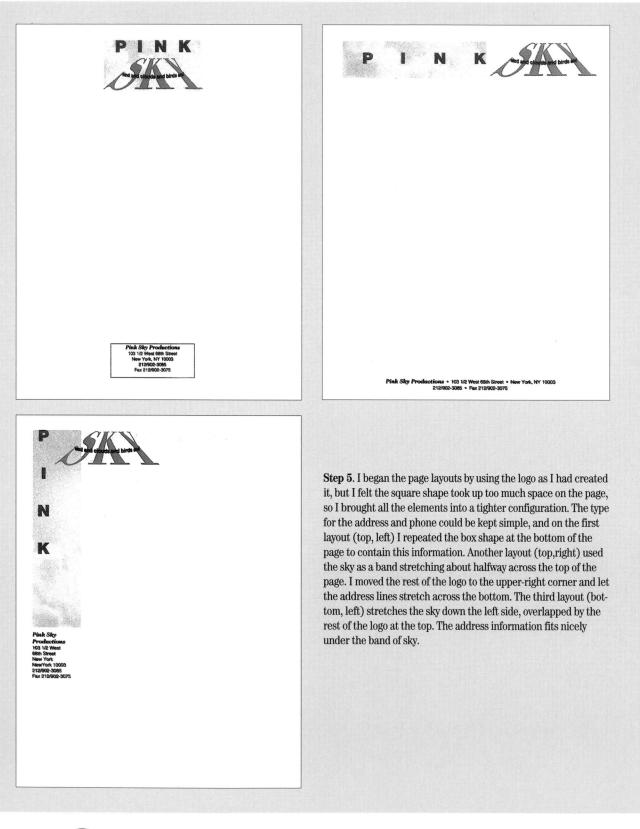

Step 5. I began the page layouts by using the logo as I had created it, but I felt the square shape took up too much space on the page, so I brought all the elements into a tighter configuration. The type for the address and phone could be kept simple, and on the first layout (top, left) I repeated the box shape at the bottom of the page to contain this information. Another layout (top,right) used the sky as a band stretching about halfway across the top of the page. I moved the rest of the logo to the upper-right corner and let the address lines stretch across the bottom. The third layout (bottom, left) stretches the sky down the left side, overlapped by the rest of the logo at the top. The address information fits nicely under the band of sky.

Images

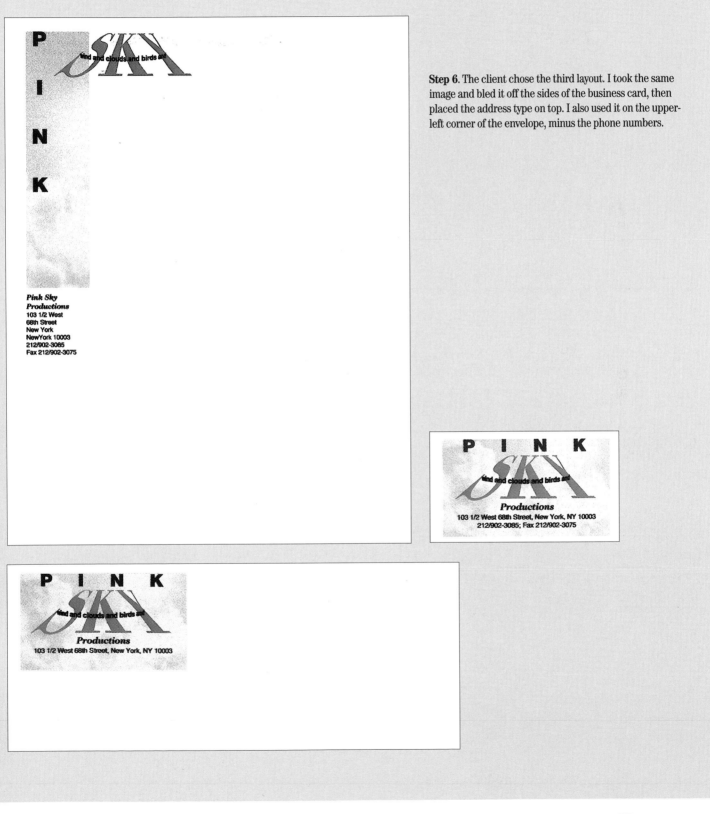

Step 6. The client chose the third layout. I took the same image and bled it off the sides of the business card, then placed the address type on top. I also used it on the upper-left corner of the envelope, minus the phone numbers.

Chapter Three
Business Card Design

"Do you have a card?" is one of the most common phrases in modern conversation. Business cards not only offer information—at least name, address and phone number—but they also provide the recipient with an instant sense of the bearer's identity. A card can be serious, calm, funny, loud, bizarre or pretty—in other words, it can have as much individuality as its owner. Business cards are traded, collected, admired and, most important, used.

The act of giving out an informative card has been with us for centuries. In the days before telephones, leaving a calling card was accepted social practice. And having a card with an office address was a simple way for a doctor or lawyer to convey service information.

We still use business cards in these ways and more. On a personal level, giving out your card is an easy way of telling someone how to contact you. And business-wise, there is hardly a company, large or small, that does not have a card. Business cards are practical; a potential customer or client won't have to scramble to write down information on a napkin or matchbook. They are user-friendly; it's easy to stick a card in a file or a Rolodex for future reference. And they can be aesthetically pleasing—a miniature design statement. They're an easy, inexpensive way to convey who you are and what you do.

Learn how to design business cards that won't get lost in the shuffle.

Layouts and Folds

In the past, the classic business card used one of several conservative layouts. One option was a large headline, company name or banner spread across the top of the card, with the rest of the information set smaller and centered beneath it, often toward the bottom of the card. Another option was to have all of the text flush left (perhaps with a logo in the upper-left corner) or, less frequently, to have all of the text flush right.

While these standard business card layouts are still common, it's now acceptable for designers to be more creative when laying out business cards. It may even be necessary to be more innovative in some cases, especially since, in our competitive society, the more unusual a card is, the more likely it is to be remembered. As long as the necessary information is provided and the card is readable, its visual effects can take as many directions as the imagination can provide.

The standard size for a business card is 2" x 3½". The standard margin is ⅛" to ¼" all around, to allow the printer flexibility in printing and trimming. If an image or color goes all the way to the edge of the card (bleeds off of it), this also means the printed area must be larger and hence use more paper, which costs more.

Type can be centered, flush left or flush right, arranged in step fashion, or placed in conjunction with a logo or graphic. Type is usually placed horizontally on a card, but using a vertical layout instead can create a fresh and creative look. The most important factor is the readability of the type; the space on a business card is

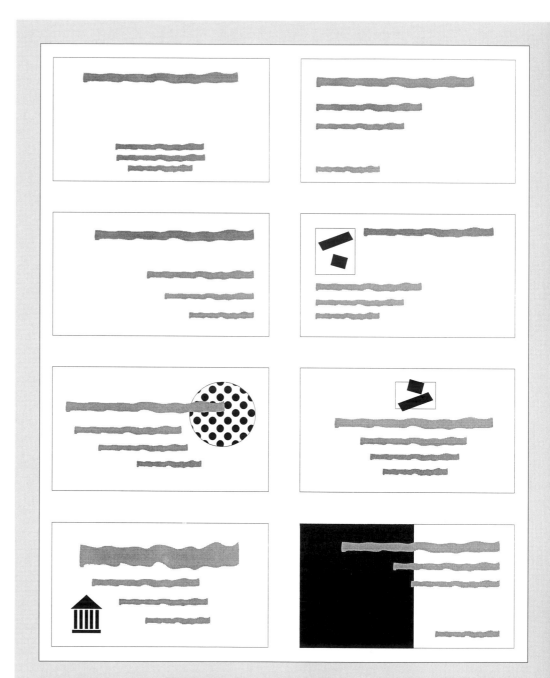

A business card with a classic layout may have type that is centered or placed to one side or the other (flush left or flush right). If a logo is used, it will typically be in the upper-left corner of the card. More innovative layouts might relate the type to a graphic or color in almost any way imaginable, as long as the necessary information is provided and the card is readable.

small, but that does not mean the type should be so minuscule that one needs a magnifier to read it.

A card can be printed on one or both sides, or it can even be made oversized and folded if there is a great deal of information that must be included. The most common fold is a 4" x 3½" card folded in half across the top edge. This provides a decorative front panel as well as plenty of extra room inside. Another common folding option is folding a 3½" x 3½" card so the top panel falls ½" short of the bottom edge. This is especially effective if the card is printed in a color or pattern on one side, with a contrasting color of paper or ink inside.

Cards are also sometimes folded in half vertically, or they may be folded twice into a *Z* shape. Another innovative option is to print a circular card and fold it in half. While cards such as these can be effective from a design standpoint, they may be awkward to carry or store in conventional card holders. When designing a business card, you will almost always have to keep a balance between creativity and practicality.

Business card folds (left column, from top to bottom): a plain standard business card, 2" x 3½"; a 4" x 3½" card, folded in half across the top edge; a 2" x 5¼" card folded vertically so the left flap folds to the middle of the card; and a vertical fold (into halves). (Right column, from top to bottom): a 3½" x 3½" card folded across the top (note that the top panel falls short of the bottom edge); a Z-shaped card, created with two vertical folds; and a vertical card, 5" x 2", with a horizontal fold that forms a top flap.

Type and Graphics

The simplest type approach on a business card is to use a single typeface in different sizes or weights. The company name, logo and/or other heading material is usually the largest point size or boldest weight, while the address, phone and fax numbers, and person's name and title are set in smaller point sizes or lighter weights. There are many faces (Garamond and Futura are just two examples) that come in a wide range of weights.

On the other hand, using two contrasting faces makes it easy to separate levels of information. One option is to combine a serif and a sans serif face. Or use a larger decorative typeface for the company name (or your own name), with a smaller, contrasting face for the address and phone number. For example, a classic choice of this kind might have a script or an italic typeface for the name and a sans serif typeface for the rest, while a more adventurous card might use hand-lettering or turn the name into a type-based logo.

Type can be fancy or plain, and even curved, bent or otherwise distorted (always keeping in mind, of course, that your primary purpose is to communicate—so keep important information legible). Most typefaces can be given a drop shadow, used in outline form, or given a fill or pattern. Explore several graphic type treatments before you select the one you think best captures the character of your own or your client's business. (See project 1 on pages 10-11 for an example of this process.)

Although type alone can be quite effective, an attractive graphic element is often the first thing someone notices about a business card—and is often what they remember when

River Contractors

210 River Road
Edgewater, NJ 07020

Michael Smith   **201-332-8576**

River Contractors

210 River Road
Edgewater, NJ 07020

Michael Smith   **201-332-8576**

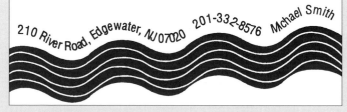

RIVER CONTRACTORS

210 River Road, Edgewater, NJ 07020   201-332-8576   Michael Smith

(Top) A traditional business card layout, where all the type is set in the same face (Times Roman) and centered, with different weights and sizes used to convey the relative importance of the information presented. For example, the headline is set the largest and in a heavier weight. (Middle) Here the headline is set in a bold italic typeface (Cochin), with a rule placed below the name. (Bottom) The card changes radically with the addition of a simple graphic. I drew a wavy black area in a drawing program, then drew some freehand white lines to place over it to simulate a river. I then used the "fit text to a path" command to get the type to duplicate the same shape as the graphic. The headline is kept very simple (Helvetica Condensed caps) to stay in balance with the graphic.

they want a product or service. Graphics should be chosen with great care; they must instantly and directly communicate something about the client or the business. And on a business card they must do this in a relatively small space.

A graphic element on a business card can be anything from a dotted line to a very representational illustration or photograph to an abstract symbol or pattern. It can be line art, digital art or a halftone. A lot of visual mileage can be achieved with rules, ornaments, clip art images or other simple graphics. Designs can be invented using cut paper, markers, watercolors or other art mediums. You can use die-cuts, embossing or foil-stamped printing methods. However, keep in mind that the more involved the graphics and the more colors you use, the more costly the printing will be, so make sure that your design can be reproduced within the client's budget.

If you are designing a business card as part of a complete letterhead system, certain constraints apply. Envision all the pieces as a unit—it's easier to make sure your design works in the rough-sketch stage than it is when you're making a mechanical. Even if you're asked to design a business card alone, keep in mind that your design might eventually apply to other pieces; try to visualize how the card's design could be adapted to other formats such as stationery, forms or labels.

A selection of business cards showing various uses of type and graphics. Clockwise from top left: The elegant, yet somewhat unusual treatment of the initial W is the center of attention here; a card using stripes, solids and shapes to good effect; a classic look, achieved with a simple, straightforward type treatment, is enlivened with a loose, freestyle logo; a playful, type-based logo gives just the right touch of creativity to this otherwise businesslike card; and a fanciful pictorial card made from cutout shapes.

Project 8: Design a Type-Based

The Client: John Lewis is an electrician who had worked for a large company for several years and was now ready to start his own business with a small client base.

John's budget was small and he wanted to stay with a black-and-white card. My strategy was to design a card that would suit his type of business, appeal to his clients, and stand out visually in a file or a Rolodex. I also wanted a card that could be printed at a quick printer or even photocopied on an inexpensive stock.

The most obvious solution was to make some sort of "electric" black-and-white logo. However, since I wanted the focus to stay on the company's name — Lewis Electric — and to make that the memorable visual, I began by experimenting with unusual type treatments of the word *electric* rather than designing a graphic element. Using black and white became a challenge rather than a limitation once I began to think about the word *electric*. Lightning flashing through a night sky is a black-and-white image, as is current running through a wire; both these ideas could be applied to a typeface.

Step 1. My first step was to play with the word electric to see how it might be depicted to suggest a lightning bolt, an electric charge, or some other type of movement. I chose a heavy weight of Helvetica Condensed and filled the word with different effects—stripes, shadows, even a lightning bolt cutting across the type. I also tried a typeface that, by its nature, is more "electric" or dynamic—in this case, a font called Technical (third from the top). I then gave it a 60 percent drop shadow. But I decided that this treatment would be effective only in two colors; since this piece was to be black and white, I concentrated on my other options. The type-fill effects were done in a drawing program on the computer, but they could also have been achieved manually by working in a large type size and by adding the stripes with narrow white tape (available in any graphics-supply store as white rule). I showed these effects to the client, who preferred the narrow stripes shown at top (white letters with a black-stripe fill and no outline). He liked the way the generous amount of white space gave a vibrating optical effect.

Business Card

Step 2. I decided the optics would work even better if the word were positioned half in and half out of a black field. I drew a black rectangle to bleed ⅛" off three sides of the card. This split the card in two — a black top and a white bottom. When I placed the striped lettering in the midsection of the card, it made the word look quite vibrant.

Step 3. The whole name of the company is Lewis Electric. Setting the word *Lewis* in heavy white letters and placing it on the black field gives it enough weight to be seen and remembered, even though the 24-point type is roughly half the size of that of *electric*. The letters are evenly spaced across the card so they run the same width as the display type.

Step 4. The final step is to add the address and phone number in 7-point Univers Light. The lines of the address are extended to space the type across the full width of the card. This gives the card visual balance. The final card was appropriate for the type of business it represented, and it would certainly stand out in anyone's file or Rolodex.

Specifications:

Hardware: PC 386

Software: CorelDRAW

Type:
"Electric": 65-point Helvetica Condensed
"Lewis": 24-point Univers Black
All other type: 7-point Univers Light

Color: One, black

Paper: White card stock

Size: 2" x 3½" with a three-sided bleed

Things to do with type on a business card:

- Use company initials as a monogram.

- Emphasize different information with different type weights.

- Make the first letter of each word larger or heavier.

- Consider using type-fill effects in place of graphics.

- Change one letter to a geometric shape.

- Change the spacing between letters to either very tight or very loose.

- Use color to emphasize certain words, such as a name.

Project 9: Using Graphics in a

The Client: Annie, of Annie's Tiles, is a craftsperson who creates hand-made ceramic tiles. Annie's tiles are mostly geometric patterns in pastel colors. Her designs are loosely based on classic patterns from the turn of the century, such as the black-and-white patterns used in old-fashioned bathrooms. The business was built by word of mouth; Annie started by producing tiles for herself and friends, and gradually people began asking her for commissioned work. Her company name evolved from the fact that people would recommend "Annie's tiles."

Annie had never advertised or had any kind of card or letterhead. She wanted a card that related to the tiles she makes, quickly identifying her business yet remaining fairly abstract. Annie felt that having a card in color was a priority because her work was in color, so spending the extra money on printing was not an issue. She thought that at some time in the near future she would want stationery and envelopes as well. We decided to play with the idea of using an overall pattern that would be tile-like, yet also stand on its own just as a pattern.

Step 1. I began by experimenting with some shapes that might make a pleasing pattern. These are all from the Zapf Dingbats typeface available on most computers, but if you're not working on a computer, you could use shapes and patterns from clip art books. I picked a few shapes that were close to those actually used in Annie's tile work, such as diamonds and triangles. Then I repeated each one a few times, using spaces between the items and adjusting the leading between lines to make a pleasing pattern.

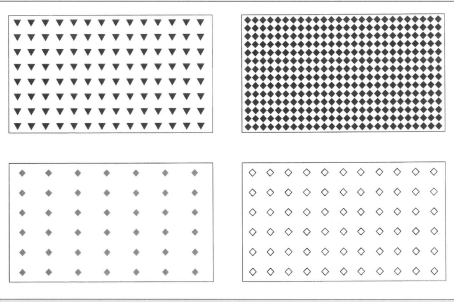

Step 2. The client preferred using a diamond shape, so the next step was to see how various repeat patterns would work in a business card-size format. I drew a standard business card-size box (2" x 3½"), then used the copy and paste keys on the computer to fill the box with a dingbat repeat. I used this process with the other diamond repeats, varying the space and leading between motifs, and showed the results to Annie. She wanted to use the diamonds in an even pattern because that was more tile-like.

Business Card

Specifications:

Hardware: Macintosh IIci

Software: QuarkXPress

Type:
"Annie's Tiles": 24-point Kabel Black
All other type: 12-point Kabel Regular

Colors: PMS 322 teal and PMS 715 salmon

Paper: 65# white recycled

Size: 2" x 3½" with a four-sided bleed

More innovative ways to use graphic elements:

- Arrange a series of rules to form a larger graphic element.

- Set information in one area off from another area with a border.

- Repeat a motif — such as leaves — under a title.

- Use a single dominant graphic rather than several small ones.

- Illustrate a product or service with line or continuous-tone art.

- Create a symbol from geometric shapes.

Step 3. I redrew the diamond pattern, then repeated it in various ways and applied colors. The type treatment needed to be simple and direct to contrast with the busy pattern. I tried a few different type approaches on several diamond background patterns. Placing the type directly over the pattern seemed busy and confusing, so I placed the type in a white box, which brought back some balance.

Step 4. In the end, the card that was the most harmonious was the simplest—an even pattern of allover diamonds, covered by the white box with a narrow rule all around to contain the type.

Project 10: Combining Type and

The Client: One aspect of Patricia's business—buying antique and decorative items to use as containers for her plants and flowers—requires using business cards quite a bit. She regularly scours flea markets, junk and yard sales, and antique stores for such pieces, and every time she purchases an item, she also gives the merchant her business card. In addition, she gives out her card to prospective clients at both business and social gatherings. She also looks for local outlets that might sell her creations, and these merchants need a card from her, too. Hence she felt she needed to print more business cards than letterhead, envelopes or invoices.

When printing in color, the more you print, the more cost-effective the job becomes, so we decided to print three thousand cards. The mechanical for the printer was done so twelve cards could be printed on one 8½" x 11" page. One version of the card was left without a name so anyone working for Pink House Design (Patricia occasionally uses freelance help) could also use the cards.

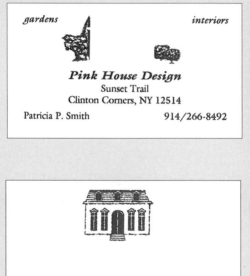

Step 1. The business card that Patricia had been using (left) was simple and quite nice; the little ornament and the type are in green, and the paper is a buff color. The new card, using the newly created logo, will also use green type, but a darker, grayer green. The house will be printed in pink, like it is on the letterhead, (see project 5) and the bushes will be in the same green as the type. The paper will be a heavier weight of the white paper used in the letterhead.

Step 2. (Above) I tried several different layouts for the card. I had saved and imported the Pink House logo as an EPS file and therefore could scale it easily to any size. For this business card, I decided to use the logo at about 65 percent of the size it was used on the letterhead. In the end, we chose the third variation of the card — with the logo and address just above center and the name Pink House Design placed under the graphic, as it was for the letterhead. The words *gardens* and *interiors* were used in the upper-right and -left corners to quickly convey the nature of the business.

Step 3. (Above) Color is already specified in the graphic, but for the mechanical (the final, camera-ready pages to be supplied to the printer), both the type and the logo must be separated according to the colors they will print. So the pink house will go on one plate and the type and green bushes will go on another plate.

Existing Graphics

The Assignment: Create a business card for Pink House Design to go with its logo and letterhead .

Step 4. The actual mechanical has twelve cards on one sheet, with crop marks at the edges. This is the base (green) plate. There is an additional plate for the red (pink house). The printer cuts the cards following the crop marks. This makes maximum use of the 8½" x 11" paper stock and saves money.

Step 5. The final card is an appropriate addition to the Pink House Design letterhead system. (The letterhead and envelope are shown in Project 5, pages 56-59.) It's eye-catching since it's printed in two colors, and it expresses both the type of business offered as well as the origin of the business name.

Specifications:

Hardware: PC 386

Software: Aldus PageMaker, Corel-DRAW

Type: Galliard Bold and Galliard Light

Colors: PMS 198 deep pink, PMS 576 dark green

Paper: Nekoosa Natural Offset cover stock

Size: 2" x 3½"

Ideas for using color on a business card:

- Print the background in a solid color and allow the type to reverse out to the color of the paper.

- Print the back of the card in a colored pattern.

- Use a colored frame that bleeds off every edge of the card.

- Create a brushstroke, using brush and ink, to use as an underline.

- Use one regular ink color and one metallic color.

- Print a background color in a tint that fades from top to bottom or side to side.

Project 11: Color Graphics and

The Client: Christopher Otis works for a large real estate firm that provides him with a very conservative business card that is appropriate for his business life but less appropriate for his personal life; thus he wanted a card that was more fun for personal use. In describing what he wanted, Chris used terms such as "colorful," "musical," "vibrant," "interesting" and "technological." And he wanted to use his favorite color, teal blue. But he didn't want something that looked silly or juvenile.

The card didn't need a lot of information — just name, address and phone number. Chris didn't have any particular type of logo or graphic treatment in mind, so I was free to experiment with any type of treatment I could think of. Budget wasn't an issue either, so I could use color, bleeds and extra printing techniques, but he did want to stay with a one-sided, standard-size card as it's easy to carry around.

Chris's nickname is his initials, "CO." I liked the roundness of these letters, and I also liked the idea of focusing on his nickname, so I decided to design a card that took advantage of those two factors.

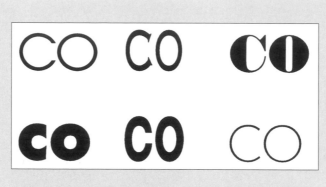

Step 1. I began "sketching" directly on the computer. I knew I wanted to work with the initials *C* and *O*, so I started by placing them on the page in 60-point Avant Garde, then repeating them in several other typefaces: Copperplate Condensed, Falstaff, Futura Black, Grotesque Condensed and Geometric. I wanted to see the shapes that these letters made and how these shapes might fit on a card. I liked the weight of the Futura Black type and thought it would translate well into a graphic shape.

Step 2. Since I knew I would be working with color, I thought the simplest type would be the most effective. I chose 60-point Futura Black and placed one blue and one brown letter in an outline the size of the card. Changing the size and the configuration of the letters gave me a good sense of how I might change the shape of the card to suit the initials.

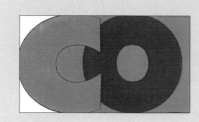

Step 3. I made the letters even rounder and added a background tint the same color as the *C* to form the shape of the die-cut on the left-hand edge of the card.

Creating Logos & Letterheads

a Diecut

The Assignment: Make a card that takes full advantage of color and printing technique; in this case, a diecut.

Step 4. To get the effect of a three-color job using only two ink colors, I reversed out the type so that it would appear white, the color of the paper. So, once again, the simpler the better in terms of type readability. I chose 9-point Futura Black caps for the name because it gave the line of type a solid, chunky feel. For the phone number (11-point Futura Medium), I set the line of type, then drew a circle the size of the *O*. I used the "fit text to path" command to curve the type, so it fit nicely along the right-hand edge of the *O*. The address, in 8.5-point Futura, is condensed to suit the shape inside the *O*. I also enlarged the size of the *O* until the type fit nicely inside.

Step 5. The final step was to add some decoration—a dot and several lines in white—that would lead the eye to the pertinent information on the card. For the printer, the left edge of the keyline is removed on the mechanical, and the die-cut is marked to follow the outline of the *C*. The end result is a card with a look that's modern enough to reflect the vibrancy and informality Chris wanted, but classic enough to stand the test of time.

Specifications:

Hardware: PC 386

Software: CorelDRAW

Type:
Initials C and O: 60-point Futura Black (manipulated)
Name: 9-point Futura Black caps
Address and phone number: Futura Medium

Colors: PMS 549 blue, PMS 476 dark brown

Paper: White coated card stock

Size: 2" x 3½" with a four-sided bleed and a die-cut on the left side of the card

Advanced business card graphics:

- Print on the front and the back of a card.

- Use a fold and a die-cut to make color from the inside show through to the outside when the card is folded.

- Print a metallic foil over a logo.

- Give the card a saw-toothed edge with die-cutting.

- Blind emboss a geometric shape and wrap the type around it.

- Place type over a four-color photograph.

Chapter Four
Business Form Design

The goal of a business form is to collect or dispense information in a logical, systematic way. A well-planned form organizes large amounts of information or complicated pieces into manageable areas. It clarifies necessary data and makes it easy to find a small detail in the midst of a lot of other words or numbers.

Forms, therefore, need primarily to be clear and useful. Secondly, they need to be nice to look at. While it's not simple to design an attractive and effective form, it can be done with a little extra time and effort. And there's additional incentive to having a good-looking form: People are more likely to respond to it (by paying an invoice, for example) and to use it (by filling out an order form).

The design of business forms has often been overlooked by the companies that use them, and even by creative professionals themselves, but they are a definite promotional opportunity and should be designed with the same care as letterhead or business cards. While it may seem easier and cheaper to use a mass-produced form (and many types are available through your local stationery store), this will deprive you—or your client—of a cohesive stationery system, as well as a valuable chance for self-promotion, and may end up costing you income rather than saving you money.

> Learn how to design business forms that will get noticed— and get used.

Organizing a Form

Almost every modern business uses a variety of forms that often need updating as a company changes and grows. When designing a form, the first thing to think about is what needs to be included on each page. Once this is established, you can begin to consider how to visually organize the material. Your first priority is making sure the client has included all pertinent information on the form. Having one small but crucial item missing can create havoc. An invoice, for example, is not complete without the company's name, address, phone number and fax number; the client's name, address and phone number; and the invoice date, order number or job number, a job description, costs, total amount due and terms of payment.

It's a good idea to put a form through some tests before you print it in mass quantities. Ask friends or colleagues to use the form and return it to learn how complete (and how useable) it is—or to determine if the wording or the arrangement of material could be misunderstood by those who will use the form.

Another good safeguard is to compare the form you're designing to other forms of its kind to make sure you haven't omitted anything. For instance, a quick glance at a catalog's order form might remind you that yours is missing a line for the expiration date of the customer's credit card. If you design business forms regularly, you might even want to start accumulating a file of forms you think especially suit their intended purpose, or simply look really great.

Once you have the right information, the next challenge in designing a form is making all the elements fit

Thumbnail sketches illustrate how the information on a form can be arranged on a page. Possibilities include using blocks of copy, columns or rows, headings, and/or shapes and color to separate areas of copy.

Facsimile Transmittal Cover Sheet

Date: _____

Number of pages (including this page): _____

To:

From:

STAR

Comments:

A simple fax transmittal form uses "color" (black boxes and gray bars) to highlight different areas of the form. Fax forms, because of the different qualities of reproduction at the fax's destination, need to be kept simple and easy to read. Adding the logo, however, helps retain the visual identity of the company.

in the designated page size, yet still have a form that is clear and easy to use. So when you have all the information you need to include in your form, step back and take a look at the density of your typed page. If you don't have much material, it won't be too hard to lay out the elements on a printed page. But if there is a great deal of copy, you will need to find ways to organize the material.

Begin by breaking the printed copy into small, logical increments. Then consider whether the form needs to be laid out with columns, boxes or other areas. Think, too, about how the form will be used. Will someone check a box, fill in a line or circle a number? Decide if areas of copy need headings or some other type of separation. Go to your sketch pad and roughly lay out how your material might fit on the page. Use boxes or shaded areas to indicate blocks of copy; use a darker pencil or a color to show headings. You can also do thumbnail sketches on the computer in essentially the same way. Make several layout variations and you will begin to see how best to use your allotted space.

The more complicated the information, the simpler the design should be in order to make the job of filling out the form easier. On a time sheet, for instance, you may be tracking the amount of time each employee spends on a job as well as how the day, week and month break down into various jobs for each person. You need to decide how small a time increment you need to track, as well as how many jobs can be tracked on the same form. Some companies find it easier to keep track of one employee's jobs each day on the same form;

Organizing a Form

others prefer keeping track of the job itself, logging in different employees and their time as appropriate.

The first time sheet illustrated (on this page) is quite simple, keeping track of one person's jobs (up to six different jobs per day) each day, for a total of four days. The second time sheet (on the next page) looks much more complex and contains a lot of information, but it is easy to fill out because keeping track of time simply involves putting a mark in a designated box — or running a line through several boxes — to indicate the day, or days, on which certain portions of a project were completed.

If there are areas of the form that people will need to fill out (and this applies to more forms than not), make sure the designated spaces are large enough to accommodate handwritten responses, since most people won't bother to type the information. If you do want typewritten responses, you may want to request them, and then make sure to design appropriately sized lines or spaces to hold typewritten information. An address area should have room for two or three lines with the lines spaced at least ¼" apart (⅜" is better) to leave room to write. If the form has columns, each column must be wide enough to accommodate any likely entry. If not, you'll find the form inadequately filled in, creating confusion and possible errors.

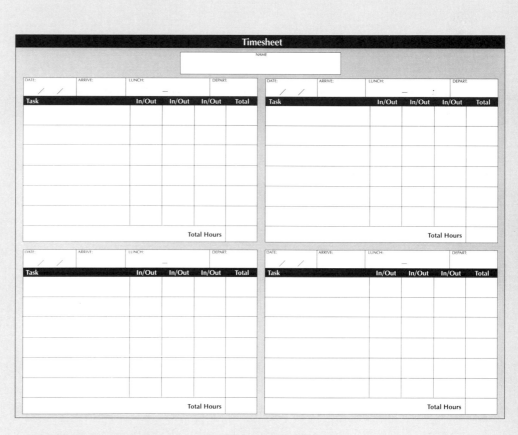

A simple time sheet, to be used by one individual, is organized by the day, leaving room for as many as six different jobs to be worked on in a four-day period.

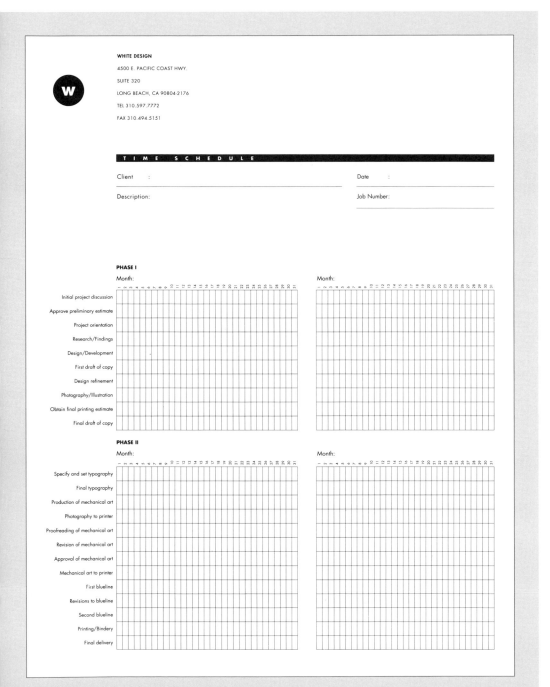

Some standard business forms are:

- receipts
- invoices
- order forms
- time sheets
- schedules
- job logs
- phone logs
- phone message forms
- fax transmittal forms
- job estimates
- service contracts
- membership forms
- entry forms
- surveys
- questionnaires
- printing orders
- checklists

This time sheet looks complex, and contains a lot of information, but is actually quite easy to fill out. Since it's organized by job, it can cover a varied amount of time. Putting a mark in the designated box — or running a line through several boxes — shows which portions of a project have been completed and when they were finished.

Type Considerations

The type on a form must first and foremost be easy to read. Generally, this means choosing a simple sans serif typeface, such as Helvetica or Frutiger, for most of the elements on the form. Use different weights of the same face to indicate levels of information. If you have a form that has very little copy, you may use a very readable serif typeface such as Century or Times Roman instead. Save any fancier type for the title or headlines.

The more copy there is and the more tiny columns or segments the form includes, the smaller (and harder to read) the type will be. Going below 8-point type is very difficult to read and better saved for footnotes (which often aren't read anyhow). Rather than continuing to decrease the size of the type, try using a condensed version of the same face. Type can be compressed by computer, but most standard sans serif typefaces are available in condensed versions. Using a condensed face is preferable to "shrinking" a regular face as it is designed to be compressed and will therefore be more readable.

Be careful of using reverse type on a form. While a bar of black containing a reverse heading can be visually arresting, if the type size is too small or the serifs too thin, the type can close up and be unreadable if the form is photocopied or faxed. Keep the type in a reverse area in a blocky, easy-to-read face that won't get lost.

A business form also needs to be designed to coordinate with the type or graphics of a company's cards or stationery. It is certainly a good idea to use the type treatment of the company name on its business forms as well. This way, the form will look like

AIR

Ship To:

Name_____

Address_____

_____

_____Zip_____

Phone (___) _____

Fax (___) _____

Payment:

☐ Check enclosed.

☐ Please bill my ___VISA___AMEX___MC.

Card # _____

Expiration Date: _____

Signature: _____

Item #	Quantity	Description	Price @	Total Price

Subtotal: _____

Sales Tax (see chart): _____

Shipping/Handling (see chart): _____

Total Amount: _____

This invoice uses one simple typeface (Frutiger) throughout, which makes the elements very readable. Design interest comes via the company logo, as well as from using boxes (some with drop shadows) to separate the areas of information.

Creating Logos & Letterheads

fX

kamah visions

Da Te |‾‾‾‾‾|

To _____

aTt n _____

F x # _____

Fr Om _____

Com PANy _____

# of pAges inC lud iNg cO veR shEet |____|

MeSS aGe _____

_____

_____

_____

_____

_____

_____

_____

_____

_____

_____

2313 frey ave venice CA 90291
310-306 7244 ph 310-306 8055 fx

An eccentric use of type characterizes this fax form, designed to be printed right off the computer. Type is used in a playful manner, mixing upper- and lowercase, overlapping letters and doubling up lines. Because of its quirky graphics, the form is memorable.

it "belongs" to the company, even if it is printed on different paper or in black and white rather than in the company colors. If the letterhead uses a typeface that might not be appropriate for the body of the form, it can be repeated on other parts of the form, at least in the title or headings (still keeping the body of the form in a simple typeface).

Good typefaces for business forms (also consider condensed/compressed versions):

- Helvetica
- Futura
- Frutiger
- Avant Garde
- Gill Sans
- Syntax
- Stone Sans Serif
- Optima
- Palatino
- Century
- Times Roman
- Bookman

Graphic Considerations

Once you have organized the information that needs to be on the form and given it a basic layout, the next step is to make the page visually interesting. This is where graphic elements can be very useful. In addition to separating information on a form into different areas, think about how to make these areas stand out. Graphic devices can be as simple as boxes, lines, bullets and borders (or as involved as creating icons or using detailed illustrations as highlights).

Think of a form as being like a game board. Bullets or arrows can indicate where to start or where to end. Columns can represent paths to follow. Color or shading can designate where to move next. (Keep tints and colors under type light so the type printed on top of it will be readable. A screen of black, for example, probably shouldn't exceed 15 percent.) Having some fun with the layout of a form will, in turn, encourage its use.

Again, think about the other components of a company's stationery system when designing its business forms. There may be elements you need to repeat, such as the logo, and there may be other considerations that are not suitable to a form. The colors and paper used in a stationery system may or may not be suitable for a business form. In addition, some companies prefer to save money by printing a form in black ink on a cheaper paper stock. Others may want the form to be printed directly from the computer. Fancy or coated papers may be interesting for a business card but won't be good for forms that need to be written on. Heavier papers may not make it through the fax machine.

This invoice repeats the humor and the graphic components of the stationery (see page 110) but changes them slightly to fit the purpose of the form (the bandit in the photo is a lighthearted way of conveying "pay up or else"). Otherwise, this form is very simple and therefore flexible. Designer: Rick Willis.

The invoice form

INVOICE #

CHANGE ORDER #

TIMBUK 2 DESIGN

DATE:

TO:

PROJECT DESCRIPTION

DESIGN

PRODUCTION/TYPOGRAPHY

OUTSIDE SERVICE

OTHER

SUBTOTAL

TAX

TOTAL

PAYMENT

AMOUNT DUE

2475
Euclid Crescent East
Upland, CA
91784
909.949.3881

A Service charge of 1.5% will be applied to all overdue balances.

A more involved invoice uses the same design, type treatment, colors
and paper as the rest of the company's stationery (see page 29). Here,
quite a lot of information is required about each job.

Add visual excitement to a form:

- Separate areas of a form with blocks of tints or colors.

- Use a dingbat, such as an arrow or pointing finger, to indicate how to move through a form.

- Add color to a black-and-white piece with markers or stickers.

- Use different weights of lines to indicate areas to write in.

- Use different kinds of lines—solid, dashed, dotted, etc.—to set off different responses.

- Create the effect of more color by printing bars or boxes with various percentages of black or a color.

- Put a screened tint behind a section to be filled out by another (with the heading "For Office Use Only," for example).

- Repeat a shape from the logo throughout the form.

- Create a border, either solid or decorative, to surround the form.

Project 12: Text and Graphics

The Client: Parker Services is a husband-and-wife team that specializes in indoor and outdoor play environments for children. Among other things, they design for babies play spaces that make the cage-like playpen obsolete, yet provide the parent or caregiver security and give the baby an interactive, colorful and wondrous little space to explore.

The Parkers eventually want to develop a logo for their business and have a stationery system designed, but they already have very simple cards and letterhead printed and their budget is very small. So they decided that the first piece they wanted was an invoice—as one of the most important functions for any beginning company is collecting money.

They wanted something that really got noticed, yet was simple to fill out, easy to read, cheerful and colorful. Since the design of the invoice would probably have some influence over future pieces, it needed to be visually flexible, with room to add a logo or a different type style in the future. Their previously printed letterhead was so simple in style that it was not an influence, nor did I have to coordinate the invoice in any way, since it was the first piece. The piece didn't need to have a lot of information; it basically needed four spaces: room for client name and address, job specifications, price, and a space for notes or comments. Each area of the form needed to be flexible, as each project, though designed from a basic module, has different elements. But primarily the invoice needed to be noticed, and the Parkers' hope was that the client would pay with a smile.

INVOICE

Parker Services
21 Drew Road, Weehawken, NJ 07087
201/389-9085

Step 1. The first step is to divide the page into separate visual areas for each information group—client information; job specifications; price of each element; comments; and company name, address and date. I began with the idea that the items that would stay the same (i.e., company name and address) would appear vertically on the page in a yellow strip, and the information that would change or need to be filled in would be set horizontally to give the page interest. I typeset the word invoice and the name and address in Frutiger—a clean, clear face that I knew would read well even on its side. I rotated the name and address and placed the type at the bottom of the yellow strip.

in an Invoice

The Assignment: Create an invoice that's colorful and playful to suit the nature of the client's business.

Specifications:

Hardware: Macintosh IIci

Software: PageMaker, LetraStudio

Type:
"Invoice" and company name and address: Frutiger
"Client," "Specifications," "Price" and "Comments": Helvetica Condensed
Remaining type: Gill Sans Condensed

Colors: PMS 123 yellow, PMS 239 magenta, and black

Paper: A bright white 20# sheet

Size: 8½" x 11"

A well-planned form should:

- Have information divided into clear, separate areas.

- Run from top to bottom and left to right—the way people read.

- Coordinate with any stationery or other printed pieces that already exist.

- Be both functional and attractive.

- Have rules that are thick enough to hold up during printing (at least 0.5 point).

- Include the client's logo, address and phone/fax information.

- Have address and phone/fax information where it can be changed without redoing the whole form (in case of relocation).

- Have dollar amounts set off with dollar signs.

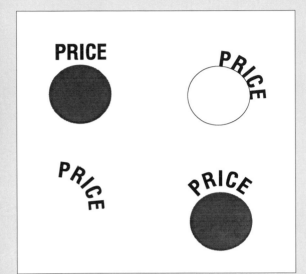

Step 2. To make the invoice more fun, I developed a marker for each major category, using a magenta circle with the category name in black text wrapping around the top. (Magenta lines were also used to separate the main categories of information.) I made the markers in LetraStudio by first drawing a circle, then filling it with color. I then typed in the word above the circle in 36-point Helvetica Condensed and used the "fit text to path" command to join the two elements so the text curved around the circle. This placed the type to the side of the circle, so I rotated the icon until the text was in the right spot. (You can combine text with a graphic in many drawing programs; check your manual for instructions.)

Step 3. I made a marker for each of the categories, then saved each finished category marker as a TIFF file to later import into my document.

Project 12: Text and Graphics in an

DATE

Step 4. Now I needed to think about the other type elements on the page. Every invoice needs a date, and I wanted to give that area a more graphic treatment. I drew a short 2-point rule and added two hairline oblique rules to separate the areas where you would fill in the date numbers. The word *date* is set in 6-point Helvetica and placed above the rule to the left. I placed this date marker below the word *invoice*.

Step 5. The four markers are added at the top left of each section, providing bright spots of color as well as playful shapes on the piece. I also decided, once the markers were in place, that the address line looked too cramped, so I moved the telephone number up to the address line, separating it with a bullet.

INVOICE

DATE:

CLIENT

SPECIFICATIONS

PRICE

COMMENTS

Parker Services
21 Drew Road, Weehawken, NJ 07087 • 201/389-9085

Invoice

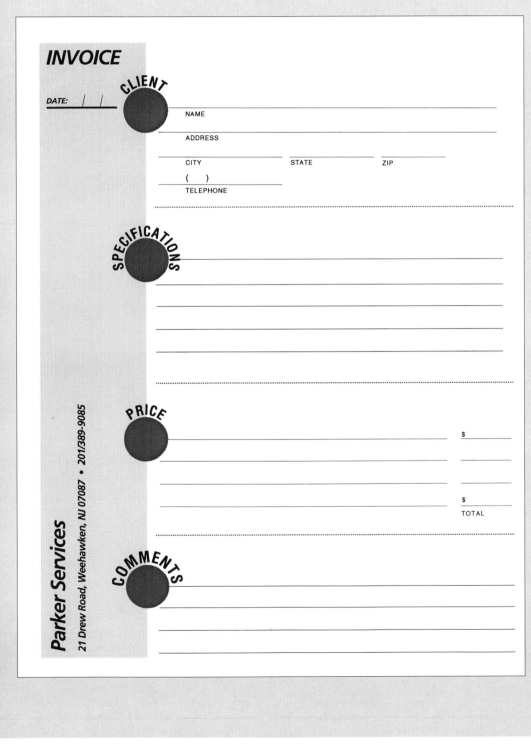

INVOICE

DATE: / /

CLIENT

NAME

ADDRESS

CITY STATE ZIP

( )
TELEPHONE

SPECIFICATIONS

PRICE

$

$
TOTAL

COMMENTS

Parker Services
21 Drew Road, Weehawken, NJ 07087 • 201/389-9085

Step 6. I also specified where to put the information under the client category, adding *name, address, city* and so on in 6-point Helvetica beneath the appropriate lines. Finally, I broke the price area into two columns, adding dollar signs and a total line.

Project 13: An Invoice to Match

The Client: Patricia Smith, of Pink House Design, wanted a form that would serve two functions: to be both an estimate sheet for the start of the job and an invoice for the conclusion. The types of jobs she does vary, from designing a simple herbal windowbox to much more elaborate garden designs, so the form needed to be flexible enough to accommodate either a lot of information or just a little. The estimate/invoice form would need space for a list of materials and labor costs. Her company has a warm and friendly feel, so she planned to handwrite when filling out the form. It would then need to be photocopied to provide duplicate copies. She wanted to use her logo as well as maintain the graphic look of the stationery, and print the form in the same colors and on the same paper.

Logo

Pink House Design
Sunset Trail
Clinton Corners NY 12514

estimate/invoice

customer name
address
telephone #

date

job description

materials
unit price/quantity/net price

labor

additional estimated expenses

total estimate/amount due

tax

Terms: A deposit of 20% of the complete job estimate must be secured before any work is begun. Final payment is required 30 days from date of invoice. A 1.5% late charge will be incurred per month for late payment.

Patricia P. Smith
914/266-8492
Fax: 914/373-8911

Step 1. The first thing I did was to make a list of everything that was needed for both the estimate and the invoice portions of the form, as well as a list of the graphic elements that would be on the page. I grouped items logically as I listed them, anticipating the division of the area into parts. Listing everything gave me a sense of how much copy I had; which items, such as the client name and address, needed to appear only once; and which items should be in which part of the form. I knew I needed to make maximum use of the page to accommodate everything.

the Letterhead

The Assignment: Design an invoice for Pink House Design to go with its new stationery and business card.

Logo

Pink House Design
Sunset Trail
Clinton Corners NY 12514

date

estimate/invoice

job description

customer name

address

telephone #

materials
unit price/quantity/net price

amount due
tax
total

labor

additional estimated expenses

total estimate

Terms: A deposit of 20% of the complete job estimate must be secured before any work is begun. Final payment is required 30 days from date of invoice. A 1.5% late charge will be incurred per month for late payment.

Patricia P. Smith
914/266-8492
Fax: 914/373-8911

Step 2. It made sense to split the page into two halves, one for the estimate and the other for the invoice, so I copied the items on the list and placed them in boxes on the appropriate sides. I used the same typeface—Galliard—that appeared on the stationery and card.

Specifications:

Hardware: PC 386

Software: Aldus PageMaker

Type: Galliard Bold and Galliard Light, various sizes

Colors: PMS 198 pink and PMS 576 dark green

Paper: Nekoosa 80# Natural Opaque

Size: 8½" x 11"

Making your business forms work with the letterhead system:

- Use the same paper stock on your business forms as used for the letterhead or card, even if the budget doesn't allow for color printing.

- Try to use the same type treatment of the company name on all parts of the system — including business forms.

- Consider using the letterhead typeface for the body of your business forms, but only if it's a simple, readable face.

- If the graphics are too involved to be repeated on the business forms, consider using just a portion of the graphics or a simplified version.

- As a minimum, try to use the client's logo, even if there's no way to include other graphic elements.

- Carry over the colors used for other parts of the system if the budget allows for this.

Project 13: An Invoice to Match the

Patricia P. Smith
914/266-8492
Fax: 914/373-8911

Date _____

Pink House Design
Sunset Trail
Clinton Corners NY 12514

Estimate / Invoice

Description of job: _____
_____
_____
_____
_____
_____

Customer

Name _____

Address _____
_____
_____

Telephone # _____

Materials

	unit price	# of items	net price
	Subtotal:		

Terms: A deposit of 20% of the complete job estimate must be secured before any work is begun. Final payment is required 30 days from date of invoice. A 1.5% charge will be incurred per month for late payment.

Remit payment to Pink House Design, Sunset Trail, Clinton Corners, NY 12514.

Labor: _____
Additional Estimated Expenses: _____
Total Estimate: _____

Amount Due: _____
Tax: _____
Total: _____

Step 3. I thought the materials and labor areas needed more space, and the amount due less space. I therefore moved the terms to the invoice side, providing room for a separate box for the labor and additional expenses. I also added the logo in the upper-left corner, and the owner's name, phone and fax numbers in the upper-right corner of the form. I had already placed the address in the upper-left corner (beneath the logo), but I decided to enlarge this text slightly to the same width as the logo above it. The client decided to add the address again in the terms box for emphasis.

Letterhead

Pink House Design
Sunset Trail
Clinton Corners NY 12514

Patricia P. Smith
914/266-8492
Fax: 914/373-8911

E s t i m a t e / I n v o i c e

Date _____   Date _____

Description of job: _____
_____
_____
_____
_____
_____

Materials

	unit price	# of items	net price

Subtotal: _____

Labor: _____

Additional Estimated Expenses: _____

Total Estimate: _____

Customer

Name _____

Address _____
_____
_____

Telephone # _____

Terms: A deposit of 20% of the complete job estimate must be secured before any work is begun. Final payment is required 30 days from date of invoice. A 1.5% charge will be incurred per month for late payment.

Remit payment to Pink House Design, Sunset Trail, Clinton Corners, NY 12514.

Additional Comments: _____
_____
_____
_____
_____
_____

Amount Due: _____

Tax: _____

Total: _____

Step 4. At this stage, the form looked too heavy and crowded, so I lightened the dividing lines from 1-point to .5-point. I also merged the boxes into one large box divided by these rules. The extra space in the right-hand column became available for additional comments. To further differentiate the two halves of the form, I shaded the invoice side in a 10 percent tint of pink. The copy and rules are printed in the same dark green as the logo. The last touch was to add an additional date line at the top of the form, as the invoice date was certain to be different from the estimate date.

The Client: Projected Images is a nonprofit organization that shows foreign, independent and alternative films. The audience has grown considerably in the six years the organization has been around, and the director, Geri Fallo, wanted a new look for the flyer and membership form, especially since they had just finished printing a new T-shirt design (a gift to every new member).

The membership form would be used in two ways: first, as a handout to be placed on the table during the actual screenings and, second, on the back of the monthly flyers sent to the mailing list to promote the upcoming films. The normal size of the mailer is 8½" x 14", with the bottom panel used as a self-mailer. The form, therefore, had to fit into an 8½" x 11" space for the mailer. For the handout, Geri wanted to use the whole 8½" x 14" and include illustrations of the various T-shirt designs. So the redesign needed to be flexible enough to work at both sizes. Since it was to be photocopied rather than printed, which usually results in a loss of type and graphic quality, the piece needed to be kept very simple.

The existing order form lacked organization, primarily because new bits of information were added as they came up and if they fit. The first thing to do was to reorder and edit the copy that needed to be included on the form. We used several old flyers and cut and pasted together the information in a more logical order, placing all the general information about the organization in one area, then having the membership information, T-shirt offer and small box to be mailed in with the membership application.

Step 1. The original flyer/membership form was a chaotic 8½" x 14" sheet. On one side were movie listings and the Projected Images logos — the main logo and the "sixth season" logo—which were designed by McKevin Shaughnessy. On the other side was a lot of information about Projected Images that seemed to change each time the form was printed. This was the side to be redesigned.

Membership Form

The Assignment: Redesign a two-sided form using an existing logo and copy.

What Is Projected Images Anyway?

Projected Images of Hudson County provides Northern New Jersey with a weekly series of alternative film screenings. These films include foreign films, independent features and shorts, avant garde and animated films, plus we periodical feature the work of local filmmakers. Our programs often include appearances and talks by filmmakers, including John Sayles, Les Blank, Tod Haynes and Bruce Sinofsky (*Brother's Keeper*). We began in the back room of Maxwell's six years ago, and recently moved to a new home.

Reels On Wheels

Through our **Reels on Wheels** series, Projected Images brings educational programs and entertainment to specific audiences, such as students, children, local community groups, and hospital patients. Some of the places our reels have wheeled to include the Meadowbrook Geriatric Center in Secaucus, Pollack Hospital in Jersey City, the Bayonne Jewish Community Center and the Hudson School in Hoboken.

Projected Images is a non-profit, tax exempt organization (your contributions are tax-deductible). Funding has been provided in part by a Block Grant from the Sate/County Partnership Program for the Arts, administered by the Hudson County Division of Cultural and Community Affairs, Robert C. Janiszewski, County Executive, and the Board of Chosen Freeholders.

Membership Infomation

As a friend of Projected Images, you play an important role in assuring our survival as a non-profit organization. There isn't any other movie house in the vicinity that shows the films we select, all chosen for their challenging content and/or exciting visual nature. We also don't charge $7–8 like a commercial movie house—our prices remain a modest $3–5 (plus you don't have to venture into Manhattan and pay tolls, parking, etc.). And being a member of Projected Images saves you even more.

As a **Regular Member**, you get $1 off the price of admission to all screenings for one year, plus the free T-shirt of your choice. As a **Deluxe Member**, you get $2 off the price of all screenings for one year, plus the T-shirt. And now we are also offering a **Best Friend Membership**. For $100 you get a card that entitles you and a friend to see all shows at a two-for-one price, and a complete set of all four T-shirts!

We Need Volunteers

Anyone interested in becoming a Projected Images volunteer, please call Geri Fallo at 201/217-4077

T-Shirt Designs

We have two new T-shirt designs to add to our roster of Projected Images wear created by Peter Cunis, a Hoboken artist whose work has been widely published on book and album covers, in magazines and other publications and on Henry Rollins' T-shirt. We continue to offer the Pat Longo "5,000 Fingers of Dr. T" design and we are reissuing the Jim Ryan (who now has a nationally syndicated comic strip called "Guy Stuff") T-shirt that started it all years ago. All the T-shirts are 100% cotton and come in sizes Large and Extra Large. They can be ordered by mail for $8 (plus shipping/handling) using the coupon below; purchased at any film screening for $6; provided free when you become a member!

Please make me a Projected Images member

- Regular member: enclosed is my check for $15
- Deluxe member: enclosed is my check for $25
- Best Friend: enclosed is my check for $100
- T-shirt only: enclosed is my check for $8 (includes shipping)

T-Shirt Options
Design: ___Cunis (p) ___Cunis (g) ___Longo ___Ryan
Shirt Size: ___Large ___Extra Large

Name_____
Address_____
State_____ Zip_____

Make check payable to **Projected Images**
Mail to:
Geri Fallo, 520 Jefferson Street, Hoboken, NJ 07030

Step 2. The first step was to reorganize the information into more logical chunks. I used my word processing program to type in all the elements on the previous forms, then rewrote and reorganized until I thought I had everything reading smoothly and in logical order. I then brought the document into the layout program, placed the copy in two columns, and made the body type 11-point Helvetica and the headlines 12-point Helvetica Condensed. I also used smaller point sizes of Helvetica and Helvetica Bold as needed.

Please make me a Projected Images member

- Regular member: enclosed is my check for $15
- Deluxe member: enclosed is my check for $25
- Best Friend: enclosed is my check for $100
- T-shirt only: enclosed is my check for $8 (includes shipping)

T-Shirt Options
Design: ___Cunis (p) ___Cunis (g) ___Longo ___Ryan
Shirt Size: ___Large ___Extra Large

Name_____
Address_____
State_____ Zip_____

Make check payable to **Projected Images**
Mail to:
Geri Fallo, 520 Jefferson Street, Hoboken, NJ 07030

Step 3. Next we decided on making some decorative bands to separate the areas rather than just using plain black bars with reverse type. I created each band by joining a line of Zapf Dingbats to a black bar, then masking the join with a thin white bar so that only half the dingbats show over the bar.

Step 4. The next step was to reorder the mail-in membership form itself. We kept the dashed line around the box because it indicates it should be cut out and sent in. But we separated the membership type from the T-shirt options, thus making the information more readable.

Specifications:

Hardware: Macintosh IIci

Software: Microsoft Word, PageMaker

Type:
  Reversed-out heads: 12-point Helvetica Condensed
  Remaining text: Helvetica Condensed

Color: Black and white

Paper: 20# white paper

Size: 8½" x 14" and 8½" x 11"

To produce effective order, entry and registration forms:

- Leave enough space between lines for handwriting.
- Make sure the return address is clearly printed and easy to find.
- Leave more than ample room for a respondent's name and address.
- Be clear about the information needed (otherwise, you might have to guess if "BL" is black or blue).
- Group all related pieces of information; for example, set up the form so all the prices are in the same column.

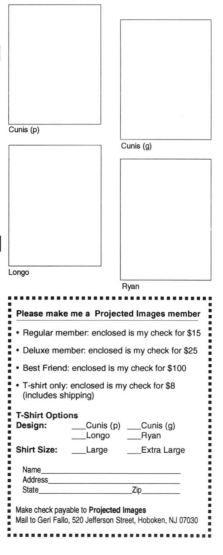

What Is Projected Images Anyway?

Projected Images of Hudson County provides Northern New Jersey with a weekly series of alternative film screenings. These films include foreign films, independent features and shorts, avant garde and animated films, plus we periodical feature the work of local filmmakers. Our programs often include appearances and talks by filmmakers, including John Sayles, Les Blank, Tod Haynes and Bruce Sinofsky (*Brother's Keeper).* We began in the back room of Maxwell's six years ago, and recently moved to a new home at **Live Tonight**, 125 Washington Street, Hoboken.

Reels On Wheels

Through our **Reels on Wheels** series, Projected Images brings educational programs and entertainment to specific audiences, such as students, children, local community groups, and hospital patients. Some of the places our reels have wheeled to include the Meadowbrook Geriatric Center in Secaucus, Pollack Hospital in Jersey City, the Bayonne Jewish Community Center and the Hudson School in Hoboken.

Projected Images is a non-profit, tax exempt organization (your contributions are tax-deductible). Funding has been provided in part by a Block Grant from the Sate/County Partnership Program for the Arts, administered by the Hudson County Division of Cultural and Community Affairs, Robert C. Janiszewski, County Executive, and the Board of Chosen Freeholders.

Membership Infomation

As a friend of Projected images, you play an important role in assuring our survival as a non-profit organization. There isn't any other movie house in the vicinity that shows the films we select, all chosen for their challenging content and/or exciting visual nature. We also don't charge $7–8 like a commercial movie house—our prices remain a modest $3–5 (plus you don't have to venture into Manhattan and pay tolls, parking, etc.). And being a member of Projected Images saves you even more.

As a **Regular Member,** you get $1 off the price of admission to all screenings for one year, plus the free T-shirt of your choice. As a **Deluxe Member,** you get $2 off the price of all screenings for one year, plus the T-shirt. And now we are also offering a **Best Friend Membership.** For $100 you get a card that entitles you and a friend to see all shows at a two-for-one price, and a complete set of all four T-shirts!

We Need Volunteers

Anyone interested in becoming a Projected Images volunteer, please call Geri Fallo at 201/217-4077

T-Shirt Designs

We have two new T-shirt designs to add to our roster of Projected Images wear created by Peter Cunis, a Hoboken artist whose work has been widely published on book and album covers, in magazines and other publications and on Henry Rollins' T-shirt. We continue to offer the Pat Longo "5,000 Fingers of Dr. T" design and we are reissuing the Jim Ryan (who now has a nationally syndicated comic strip called "Guy Stuff") T-shirt that started it all years ago.

All the T-shirts are 100% cotton and come in sizes Large and Extra Large. They can be ordered by mail for $8 (plus shipping/handling) using the coupon below; purchased at any film screening for $6; provided free when you become a member!

Cunis (p)

Cunis (g)

Longo

Ryan

Please make me a Projected Images member

• Regular member: enclosed is my check for $15

• Deluxe member: enclosed is my check for $25

• Best Friend: enclosed is my check for $100

• T-shirt only: enclosed is my check for $8 (includes shipping)

T-Shirt Options
Design: ___Cunis (p) ___Cunis (g)
___Longo ___Ryan

Shirt Size: ___Large ___Extra Large

Name_____
Address_____
State_____Zip_____

Make check payable to **Projected Images**
Mail to Geri Fallo, 520 Jefferson Street, Hoboken, NJ 07030

Step 5. I reversed out the heads and placed the fancy dividers over them. I also made boxes for the T-shirt art and for the Projected Images logos, which I planned to move to the back of the form with the other PI information, leaving more room on the front for the movie listings.

What Is Projected Images Anyway?

Projected Images of Hudson County provides Northern New Jersey with a weekly series of alternative film screenings. These films include foreign films, independent features and shorts, avant garde and animated films, plus we periodical feature the work of local filmmakers. Our programs often include appearances and talks by filmmakers, including John Sayles, Les Blank, Tod Haynes and Bruce Sinofsky (*Brother's Keeper*). We began in the back room of Maxwell's six years ago, and recently moved to a new home at **Live Tonight**, 125 Washington Street, Hoboken.

Reels On Wheels

Through our **Reels on Wheels** series, Projected Images brings educational programs and entertainment to specific audiences, such as students, children, local community groups, and hospital patients. Some of the places our reels have wheeled to include the Meadowbrook Geriatric Center in Secaucus, Pollack Hospital in Jersey City, the Bayonne Jewish Community Center and the Hudson School in Hoboken.

Projected Images is a non-profit, tax exempt organization (your contributions are tax-deductible). Funding has been provided in part by a Block Grant from the Sate/County Partnership Program for the Arts, administered by the Hudson County Division of Cultural and Community Affairs, Robert C. Janiszewski, County Executive, and the Board of Chosen Freeholders.

Membership Infomation

As a friend of Projected images, you play an important role in assuring our survival as a non-profit organization. There isn't any other movie house in the vicinity that shows the films we select, all chosen for their challenging content and/or exciting visual nature. We also don't charge $7–8 like a commercial movie house—our prices remain a modest $3–5 (plus you don't have to venture into Manhattan and pay tolls, parking, etc.). And being a member of Projected Images saves you even more.

As a **Regular Member,** you get $1 off the price of admission to all screenings for one year, plus the free T-shirt of your choice. As a **Deluxe Member,** you get $2 off the price of all screenings for one year, plus the T-shirt. And now we are also offering a **Best Friend Membership.** For $100 you get a card that entitles you and a friend to see all shows at a two-for-one price, and a complete set of all four T-shirts!

We Need Volunteers

Anyone interested in becoming a Projected Images volunteer, please call Geri Fallo at 201/217-4077

T-Shirt Designs

We have two new T-shirt designs to add to our roster of Projected Images wear created by Peter Cunis, a Hoboken artist whose work has been widely published on book and album covers, in magazines and other publications and on Henry Rollins' T-shirt. We continue to offer the Pat Longo "5,000 Fingers of Dr. T" design and we are reissuing the Jim Ryan (who now has a nationally syndicated comic strip called "Guy Stuff") T-shirt that started it all years ago.

All the T-shirts are 100% cotton and come in sizes Large and Extra Large. They can be ordered by mail for $8 (plus shipping/handling) using the coupon below; purchased at any film screening for $6; provided free when you become a member!

Cunis (p)

Cunis (g)

Longo

Ryan

Please make me a Projected Images member

- Regular member: enclosed is my check for $15

- Deluxe member: enclosed is my check for $25

- Best Friend: enclosed is my check for $100

- T-shirt only: enclosed is my check for $8 (includes shipping)

T-Shirt Options
Design: ___Cunis (p)   ___Cunis (g)
            ___Longo   ___Ryan

Shirt Size: ___Large   ___Extra Large

Name_____
Address_____
State_____Zip_____

Make check payable to **Projected Images**
Mail to:
Geri Fallo, 520 Jefferson Street, Hoboken, NJ 07030

Step 6. The illustrations for the T-shirts were scanned as TIFF files. Because the artwork was made of simple cartoons, it was reproducible even when scaled down to a 2" box. When I imported the art, I rescaled the size of the boxes to accommodate the shapes of the artwork. The larger form is designed to be used as a handout; the smaller form (8½" x 11") is simply a copy of the larger piece, but without the T-shirt illustrations. This is to be used on the flyer since it leaves room for the bottom panel of the 14" paper to be used as a self-mailer.

...ages Anyway?

...n County provides ...eekly series of alterna-...ms include foreign ...nd shorts, avant garde ...eriodical feature the ...programs often include ...makers, including ...Haynes and Bruce ...We began in the back ...go, and recently moved

you get $2 off the price of all screenings for one year, plus the T-shirt. And now we are also offering a **Best Friend Membership.** For $100 you get a card that entitles you and a friend to see all shows at a two-for-one price, and a complete set of all four T-shirts!

We Need Volunteers

Anyone interested in becoming a Projected Images volunteer, please call Geri Fallo at 201/217-4077

T-Shirt Designs

We have two new T-shirt designs to add to our roster of Projected Images wear created by Peter Cunis, a Hoboken artist whose work has been widely published on book and album covers, in magazines and other publications and on Henry Rollins' T-shirt. We continue to offer the Pat Longo "5,000 Fingers of Dr. T" design and we are reissuing the Jim Ryan (who now has a nationally syndicated comic strip called "Guy Stuff") T-shirt that started it all years ago. All the T-shirts are 100% cotton and come in sizes Large and Extra Large. They can be ordered by mail for $8 (plus shipping/handling) using the coupon below; purchased at any film screening for $6; provided free when you become a member!

...heels

...s series, Projected ...ograms and entertain-...uch as students, chil-..., and hospital patients. ...have wheeled to ...riatric Center in ...Jersey City, the ...Center and the Hudson

...x exempt organization (your ...nding has been provided in ...County Partnership ...y the Hudson County ...Affairs, Robert C. ...the Board of Chosen

...fomation

...es, you play an impor-...val as a non-profit ...other movie house in ...s we select, all chosen ...nd/or exciting visual ...$7–8 like a commercial ...ain a modest $3–5 (plus you don't have to venture into Manhattan and pay tolls, parking, etc.). And being a member of Projected Images saves you even more.

As a **Regular Member,** you get $1 off the price of admission to all screenings for one year, plus the free T-shirt of your choice. As a **Deluxe Member,**

Please make me a Projected Images member

- Regular member: enclosed is my check for $15

- Deluxe member: enclosed is my check for $25

- Best Friend: enclosed is my check for $100

- T-shirt only: enclosed is my check for $8 (includes shipping)

T-Shirt Options
Design: ___Cunis (p)   ___Cunis (g)
            ___Longo   ___Ryan

Shirt Size: ___Large   ___Extra Large

Name_____
Address_____
State_____Zip_____

Make check payable to **Projected Images**
Mail to:
Geri Fallo, 520 Jefferson Street, Hoboken, NJ 07030

Chapter Five
More Good Examples

Now it's time to look at some of the stationery systems that other designers have created for themselves or for clients. The work in this chapter was selected for its range of innovative design ideas and varying levels of production complexity. Each piece is quite different from the next, but each merits special consideration for its use of type, graphics, color, paper, or simply a very good idea.

But they all share one particular recommendation—the ability to highlight the person or business the piece was designed for. They catch your eye in some particular way, encouraging you to look twice, to pay attention. And this is the aim of any well-designed letterhead or business card—getting the audience to see and remember what they have seen or read.

When you look through this chapter, think about why each piece is attractive or eye-catching. Is it because of a strong use of color? Some unusual printing technique? A creative illustration? Perhaps it made you smile because of an unusual name or some playful graphics. Think about how the piece suits the type of client it was made for, how

> Get inspired—any concept can be a good one if it captures the positive attention of its audience.

it might interest the audience that the client is trying to reach. Then think about how you can find equally interesting methods to achieve success in your own designs.

More Good Examples

It's perfectly logical to use black and white for a company called White Design. And here the use of positive and negative contrasts are highlighted by the simplicity and elegance of the design. The paper is very bright white and opaque, the black very solidly printed. The lowercase *w* centered in a circle becomes a powerful, sophisticated little logo. On the business card, the logo is enhanced by embossing. The back of each piece is a solid black, as is the envelope back and flap, which maximizes the dramatic effect. Designer: John White, Aram Youssefian.

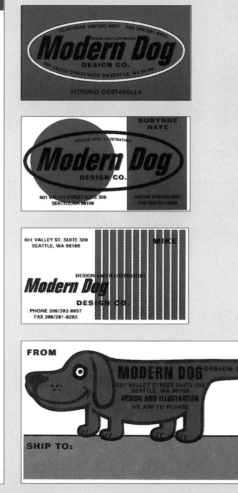

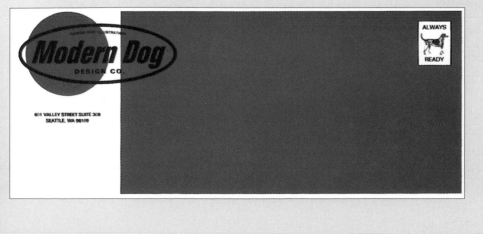

Dogs are important. I have one, and it is imperative to recognize their sense of humor (most dogs like to laugh). This design and illustration company understands and has used the concept to produce a singular look for itself—strong, funny and open to change. The colors are bright (orange, used mostly at 100 percent, and black), and the images and type treatment are strong. As the letterhead and peripheral pieces evolve, they can include new images without losing the overall feel of the stationery system or its graphic integrity. Designers: Vittorio Costarella, Michael Strassburger and Robynne Raye.

More Good Examples

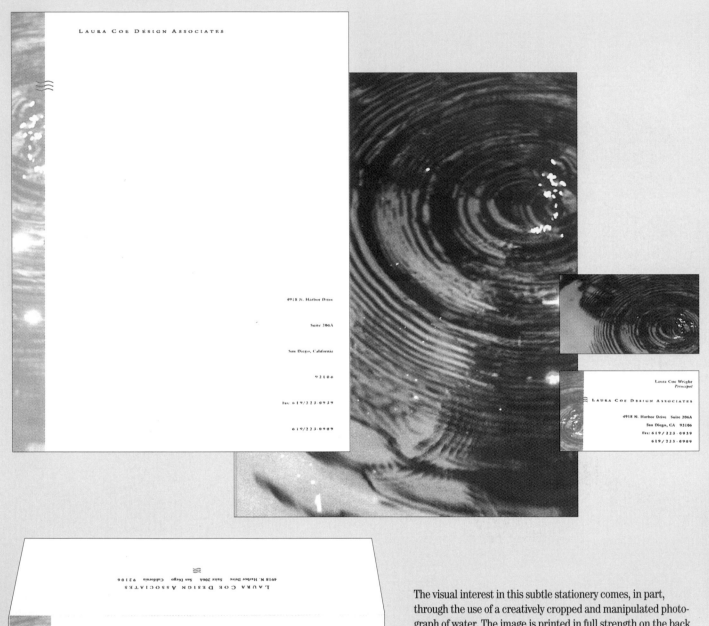

The visual interest in this subtle stationery comes, in part, through the use of a creatively cropped and manipulated photograph of water. The image is printed in full strength on the back of the letterhead and card and the inside of the envelope. It is reversed and printed in a tint as a sidebar on the front of the card and letterhead. A second color, blue-green, is used for the three fine, wavy lines that tie the image to the paper and for some of the type. The type is small and classically treated, using caps and small caps as a way to differentiate the company name from the address. Designer: Laura Coe Design Assoc.

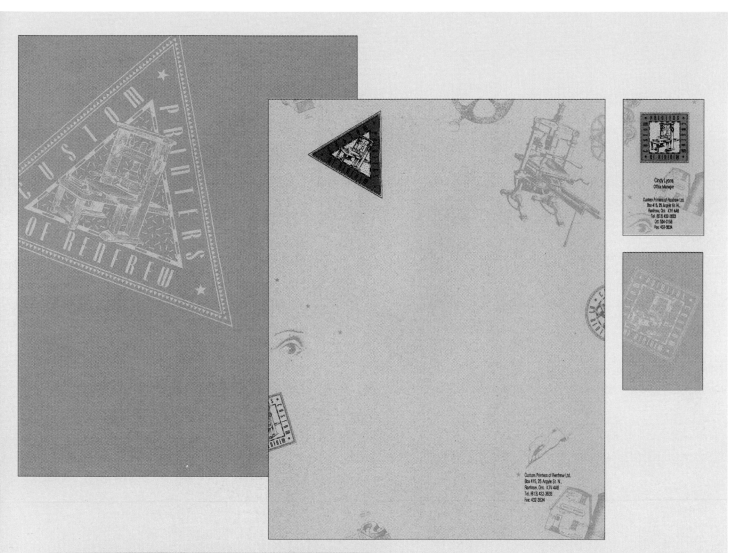

Printing companies often want to show off what they do by having an elaborate and exemplary stationery system or self-promotional items. And, since they are printing for themselves, they can afford the production costs! This letterhead is printed on a textured taupe paper with various trade images, stars, hand and eyes printed over it in tints. The designer also created several geometric logos containing the company name and an illustration of an antique printing press that float around the page. The backs of the pieces are printed in a darker taupe with large reverse logos. Designer: Terry Laurenzio.

More Good Examples

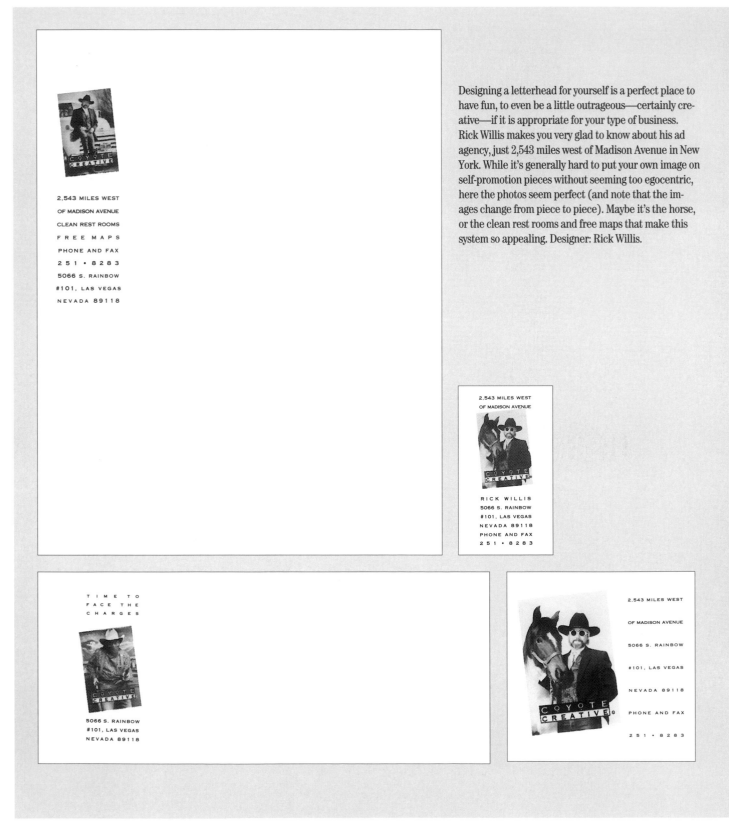

Designing a letterhead for yourself is a perfect place to have fun, to even be a little outrageous—certainly creative—if it is appropriate for your type of business. Rick Willis makes you very glad to know about his ad agency, just 2,543 miles west of Madison Avenue in New York. While it's generally hard to put your own image on self-promotion pieces without seeming too egocentric, here the photos seem perfect (and note that the images change from piece to piece). Maybe it's the horse, or the clean rest rooms and free maps that make this system so appealing. Designer: Rick Willis.

2,543 MILES WEST
OF MADISON AVENUE
CLEAN REST ROOMS
FREE MAPS
PHONE AND FAX
251 • 8283
5066 S. RAINBOW
#101, LAS VEGAS
NEVADA 89118

2,543 MILES WEST
OF MADISON AVENUE

RICK WILLIS
5066 S. RAINBOW
#101, LAS VEGAS
NEVADA 89118
PHONE AND FAX
251 • 8283

TIME TO
FACE THE
CHARGES

5066 S. RAINBOW
#101, LAS VEGAS
NEVADA 89118

2,543 MILES WEST

OF MADISON AVENUE

5066 S. RAINBOW

#101, LAS VEGAS

NEVADA 89118

PHONE AND FAX

251 • 8283

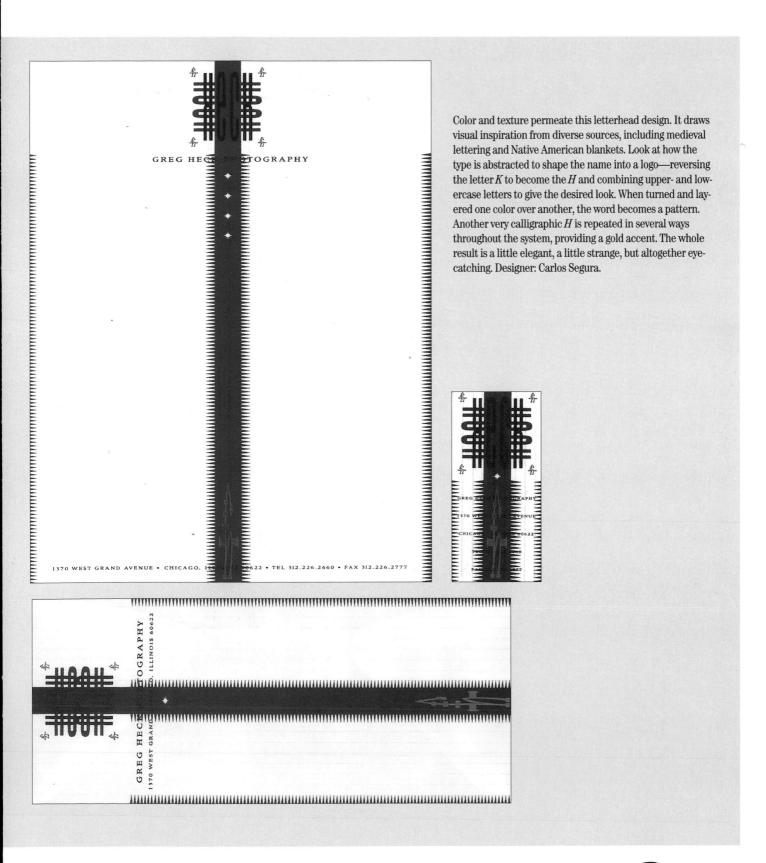

Color and texture permeate this letterhead design. It draws visual inspiration from diverse sources, including medieval lettering and Native American blankets. Look at how the type is abstracted to shape the name into a logo—reversing the letter *K* to become the *H* and combining upper- and lowercase letters to give the desired look. When turned and layered one color over another, the word becomes a pattern. Another very calligraphic *H* is repeated in several ways throughout the system, providing a gold accent. The whole result is a little elegant, a little strange, but altogether eye-catching. Designer: Carlos Segura.

More Good Examples

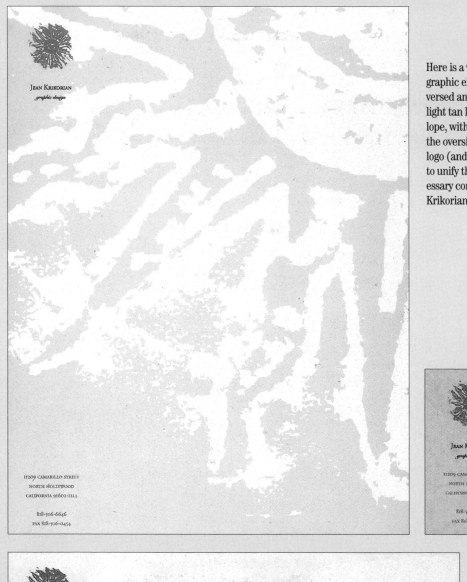

Here is a wonderful example of how to make use of a logo as a graphic element. The logo is used small, but then also reversed and printed large in blue-gray to cover most of the light tan letterhead. The light tan is used again for the envelope, with the business card in a mottled blue-gray, echoing the oversized logo on the letterhead. The copper color for the logo (and some of the type) is used throughout, which helps to unify the pieces. Black type for the name provides the necessary contrast to the otherwise muted colors. Designer: Jean Krikorian.

The Black Point Group
Design Electronique

3 Gate Five Road

Suite C

Sausalito, CA 91965

℡ 415.331.4531

FAX 415.331.6072

themook@well.sf.ca.us

Two partners, two illustration techniques, two ideas that merge and separate within one stationery system. Conceptually the treatment of the hand is quite different—one painterly and free-spirited, the other classically drawn. But both are reaching for the same ball, and hence fit together perfectly. Note, however, that the hands are separated for each partner's individual business card. Luxurious full-color printing adds to the magic. Designers: Mary Carter and Gary Priester.

The Black Point Group
Design Electronique

3 Gate Five Road
Suite C
Sausalito, CA 94965
FAX 415.331.6072
themook@well.sf.ca.us

Mary E. Carter
Partner
415.331.4531 ℡

The Black Point Group
Design Electronique

340 Townsend Street
Suite 420
San Francisco, CA 94107
FAX 415.243.8234

Gary W. Priester
Partner
Phone 415.243.8311

The Black Point Group
Design Electronique

3 Gate Five Road

Suite C

Sausalito, CA 94965

More Good Examples

This letterhead pushes the boundaries, breaks the rules, and makes for memorable design. The textured, diagonally striped paper is printed all over with bits of letters, as if the paper got chewed up along with some typewritten material and spit back out again. The company name is created three-dimensionally and photographed, dancing in and out of the shadows. It is used as a pasted-on color photo on some of the letterhead and on the envelope but printed in black and white on other pieces. The same image, printed in color, covers the front of the card, which is printed on a crinkly textured paper stock. Necessary information is simply presented on the back of the card. Designer: Carlos Segura.

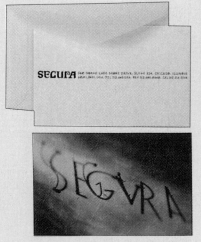

Bits of color, graphic stripes, boxes and different papers commingle to make a very flexible graphics package for this jewelry designer and gallery owner. The theme can, and does, carry through into cards, packaging and invitations. Note that not all the elements need to be used on every piece in order to maintain graphic consistency. Designer: Thomas Mann Design.

Chapter Six
Printing Basics

The last stage of designing a logo, letterhead, business card or business form is printing. This involves both choosing the type of printer appropriate for the job and preparing the artwork so the printer has all the necessary information in order to produce the piece.

Choosing a printer depends on how the finished piece will look—how many colors, what type of paper, and so on. Now, more than ever, people are printing letterhead right from their laser printers each time they write a letter or make out an invoice. For larger print quantities, or two- or three-color work, it's best to go to a commercial printer. These range from your local photocopy house, which often does offset printing, to large printers who do four-color work and/or special effects, such as embossing or engraving. A small printer will do small quantities but may not have a large paper selection; a larger printer will order paper, but only if the job is large enough to justify the purchase.

Get to know the print shops in your area. Look at the work they do. Ask how large their presses are, how many colors they handle, and

> Learn how to prepare your logos, letterheads, business cards and business forms for the printer.

what papers they stock. If you have a job to be done, bring a sample comp or dummy of the project (including indications of any artwork) so the printer sees exactly what you have in mind. Ask for price quotes and a schedule; then you can make an informed decision.

Printing Basics

Printing can be ordered using one, two, three (or more) match or spot colors of ink (also known as flat-color printing), or using color separations (known as four-color process printing). Printers have swatch books of ink colors that conform to a basic color matching system, which gives each color a coded number. (One standard is the Pantone Matching System whose colors are typically referred to as PMS colors.) You can also purchase swatch books at any graphics store. Computer drawing and layout programs have various color systems built in so you can see on screen the same colors that you will specify for the printer.

Most inks are transparent and, while darker colors will usually cover up lighter ones, there might still be some bleed-through. Medium and light colors can often be combined to make a third color. Most colors will look opaque on white paper but may not look the same on colored stock. Discuss with your printer how a color will appear in the actual piece before proceeding.

A one-color printing job uses one (match) color of ink on one color of paper—from black on white to red on mauve. It is the most affordable type of printing, with any substantial variations being in the cost of the paper. Additional match colors require additional passes through the press. It is possible to print four or five match colors, although each subsequent color adds a bit more to your printing cost.

A four-color process printing job is necessary for a full-color effect, such as you would need for any color photograph. Here the picture is separated photographically by the printer into the four basic printing colors (yellow, magenta, cyan and black). It is also possible to make color separations on the computer yourself and provide film to the printer.

Sending a job to the printer involves preparing a mechanical—a piece of flat artwork that includes everything the printer needs. The mechanical needs to be "camera ready"; that is, it must contain all the type and graphic line elements in the exact position and size that they will appear in the printed piece. Information about how to position halftones or where color goes must also be indicated, along with any folding or cutting instructions. The printer will then photograph this mechanical to make negative film for printing. Halftones are also shot, separately from the mechanical, at the size they will be printed. The resulting film is then "stripped up" into position to make a "flat," from which a printing plate is made (one for each color). Currently, the most common form of printing is offset lithography. The technology of both prepress and printing is changing very fast, however. More printers are asking for work on disk rather than in mechanical form; they can go directly from disk to film or even from disk to print.

With the advent of advanced layout programs, you can now make a mechanical completely on

This is a standard mechanical for a one-color printing job. Nonreproducible (nonprinting) blue lines are indicated here as small dotted lines. They mark the perimeter of the card and provide guides for positioning type and artwork. Crop marks are ruled in black to mark where the card will be trimmed.

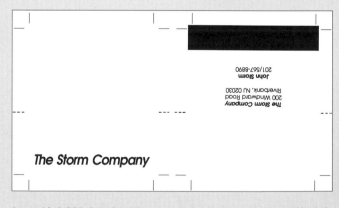

A two-sided, folded card requires two mechanicals, one for the inside and one for the outside. (Here, the outside of the card is shown on the left.) The front of the card is shorter than the back, so the black bar will show below the name. Instructions for where to fold and score the card are marked by small dashed lines.

Creating Logos & Letterheads

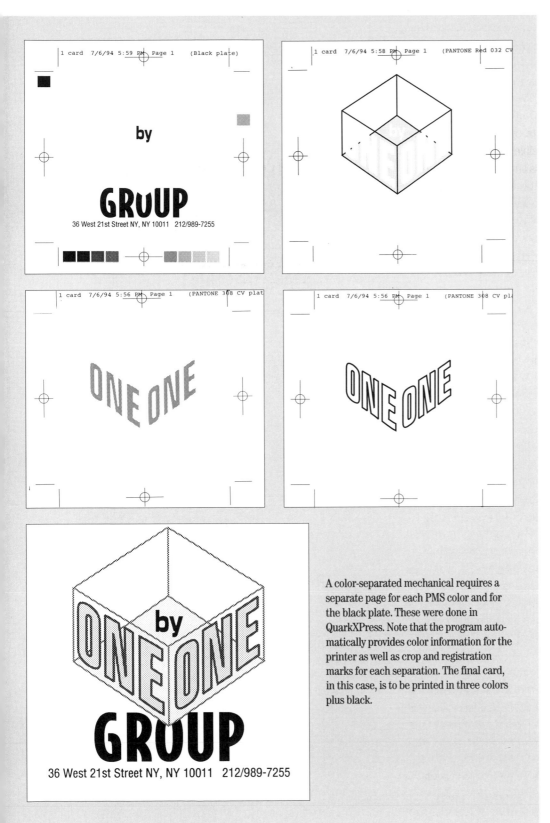

A color-separated mechanical requires a separate page for each PMS color and for the black plate. These were done in QuarkXPress. Note that the program automatically provides color information for the printer as well as crop and registration marks for each separation. The final card, in this case, is to be printed in three colors plus black.

your computer. Layout programs can provide type to size, import and position computer-generated or scanned artwork, and make rules and provide automatic crop marks—small lines at the corners of the mechanical (which stop at least $\frac{1}{16}$" short of meeting each other to ensure they stay out of the actual printed area)—that, if extended, would cross at the exact point where the piece of paper will be cut or trimmed. Your computer-generated mechanical can be sent to the printer "as is," or it can be pasted onto a slightly larger board and covered with a tissue overlay for protection. The tissue is also marked with any instructions for the printer about color, tints, and so on.

Making a mechanical completely by hand, however, is still a valid enterprise. Even if your type and graphic line art are both computer-generated, you may still have to make a mechanical to incorporate additional noncomputer elements (such as a handwritten signature or instructions for printing a tint). If you're making a mechanical by hand, you'll need to start by cutting a board (white layout or illustration board) sized a few inches larger all around than the printed piece. Then you will draw guidelines indicating the exact size and shape of the piece (the "trim") in a nonreproducible blue pen or pencil. You'll next draw crop marks in black ink at the corners of the piece to further guide the printer in trimming the piece at exactly the size you want it. Use rubber cement or wax on the back of type and other elements to paste them down in the right position.

Whether computer-generated or handmade, here are some additional

Printing Basics

guidelines for making a mechanical.

Registration marks: These are like crop marks, but they're added to the top, bottom and sides of both the mechanical and any overlays to ensure the printer lines up the artwork exactly as intended.

Photographs: Halftones (i.e., photos) are given to the printer to be shot separately, but some indication must be made on the mechanical of where to put the halftone and at what size. The most common way is to draw a holding box ("keyline") for the photo right on the mechanical. An indication of which photo to use, and at what percentage of its original size it should be shot, can then be written in the box; cropping directions should go on a tissue overlay over the photo. (If you have more than one photo, assign numbers to them. Write each number on a tag attached to the photo as well as on the mechanical—in the keyline; this safeguards against any of the photos being switched at the printer.)

For even more accuracy, have a photostat made (a low-quality halftone reproduction shot at the final size of the printed photo) that, when cropped, fits in the box. This shows which picture you want at exactly what size and how it should be positioned. Photographs can also be screened prior to printing, thus breaking up the photo into dots that can be shot as line art. This camera-ready art is pasted on the mechanical in the form of a velox (a higher-quality photostat). This can be helpful if the image is very simple or if your printer happens to be the local copy shop.

Graphic elements: Line art (art that will be printed in a solid-color ink) is placed on the mechanical in position as black-and-white artwork; the printer photographs line art right along with the type.

Colors: For flat (match) colors, either each area of color is marked on a tissue overlay on the mechanical, or the piece is actually separated into a mechanical for each color. Alternatively, acetate overlays with registration marks can also be used to add another layer to a mechanical (type, for example, that will be in a different color or tint). Computers can do this color separation for you, providing crop and registration marks on each plate. For four-color process printing, a photostat is usually provided for position on the mechanical, and the actual color art or transparency is sent to the printer for separation, along with the boards.

Folding or scoring lines: Where a piece is to be folded is indicated by a dashed line outside the printed area. If you are printing on a heavy paper stock, chances are the fold will have to be scored (lightly cut) to make the folding neater, and this should be indicated on an overlay.

Screens and tints: If you want type or line art to be printed as a screen value or tint of a solid color, it can be indicated in several ways: It can be marked on a tissue overlay; it can be prescreened by the computer; or it can be indi-

This is the original photograph of a street scene that I wanted to use for a business card. Note the clarity of the original, especially as seen in the detail.

Creating Logos & Letterheads

cated with the screened area cut from a sheet of rubylith (transparent red film on acetate) and positioned on an overlay.

Computer output: If you have typeset or created the art for your piece on the computer, you can get your output from a 300- or 600-dpi (dots per inch) laser printer, or you can send your file to a service bureau for high-quality linotronic output (usually 1200 or 2700 dpi—the higher the dpi number, the sharper the resulting image). This is more expensive than laser printing, but the higher quality of printing is worth it, especially if your art includes type or computer graphics that are small or highly detailed; remember that the higher the dpi of the output you provide, the sharper and more evenly inked your final print job will be.

If the printer is to shoot the photograph, a photostat can be made at the exact size you'll want the photo to be for the printed piece. A photostat is a lower-quality reproduction (note the difference between this and the original photo, especially in the detail), so you won't want to use it as your final artwork. Instead, paste it down where you want it on the mechanical and mark it "FPO," or "for position only." You can also just make a photocopy to use for position. Choosing a photostat versus a photocopy depends on time, budget, and how beautiful you need the mechanicals to be (whether or not they will be shown to a client).

If you want the printer to be able to shoot the image as part of the mechanical (right along with the text) you can make a velox, which prescreens the photo. You do lose image quality, however, because this process turns your halftone into dots that are shot as line art.

Index